Roughing It Easy at Girls Camp

DIAN THOMAS

DESERET BOOK

SALT LAKE CITY, UTAH

Library of Congress Cataloging-in-Publication Data

Thomas, Dian, 1945–
    Roughing it easy at girls camp / Dian Thomas.
      p.   cm.
    Includes index.
    ISBN 1-57345-962-3 (pbk.)
    1. Church camps—Church of Jesus Christ of Latter-day Saints—Management.
2. Mormon girls—Religious life.   I. Title.

BX8643.C24T48 2003
267'.8—dc21   2002156515

Printed in the United States of America   72076-6814
Publishers Printing, Salt Lake City, UT

10 9 8 7 6 5 4 3 2 1

DEDICATION

This book is fondly dedicated to my first formal and forever-favorite campsite, the Brighton Girls Camp—built in 1920 at the urging of the Liberty, Pioneer, Ensign, and Salt Lake Stakes on property located in Big Cottonwood Canyon east of Salt Lake City.

More specifically, and lovingly, this book is dedicated to the true visionaries, tireless leaders, enthusiastic counselors and staff, and all the young women who, for nearly one hundred years, have enjoyed the beauties, blessings, and bounties of the outdoors found at Brighton Girls Camp. It is my wish that campfires burn forever in the hearts of young women at Brighton and at other girls camps throughout the world.

CAMP LEADER'S PRAYER

Let me come eagerly to camp this year, Lord.
Let me come with a new delight in the countless things I must
accomplish.
Instead of my usual panic, fill me with a glowing sense of trust
and peace.
Each day that I awake, let me rejoice in the fact that I am well
and able to get up and begin.
And though there never seems to be enough time or money,
Let me remember the loaves and the fishes.
Each year there is always plenty, more than plenty.
Even time stretches out like a magic ribbon,
Somehow embracing all that must be done.
As for a woman's strength—therein lies the greatest marvel of all.
Thou givest each of us extra portions for this season so that at
the end,
We hug camp close to our hearts and don't want it to be over.
Remind me of all this as I prepare for camp this year, Lord.
Let me come eagerly to the seemingly impossible,
Knowing that this is a cause worthy of miracles.

(Adapted from a poem by Marjorie Holmes)

CONTENTS

ACKNOWLEDGMENTS

I would like to thank my parents, Julian and Norene Thomas, for giving me, as a child, an immeasurable love for the outdoors that remains with me today. Among my fondest childhood memories are the days I spent with my father, who was a forest ranger in the mountains of southern Utah. I never dreamed then that those outdoor experiences would become my lifelong passion.

I would also like to thank Vanessa Croford, Yvonne King, and Beverly Ecker—the girls camp counselors who helped make camp the watershed experience it became in my life. They will never know how grateful I am to them for introducing me to the wonders of Brighton Girls Camp.

Thanks to Shaunna Adix, director of Brighton Girls Camp from 1962 to 1965, who gave me my first job as "kitchen debutante." Thanks to Heidi Vriens, director of Brighton Girls Camp in 1966, who encouraged me to become program director for the camp. And thanks to Floss Waltman, president of the Brighton Camp Committee, with whom I serve. Floss has been a friend and camping comrade since our teenage years.

I am forever indebted to Faye B. Walch, Elayne Crockett, Betty F. Kearl, and Betty Taylor, the committee members who asked me to be director of Brighton Girls Camp.

I am also indebted to my friends at Deseret Book, notably

Eleanor Knowles, who asked me to write this book years ago, Jana Erickson, Michael Morris, Shauna Gibby, Sheryl Roderick, and Kent Minson.

I am grateful to many friends who have shared ideas and helped in the preparation of this book, including Claudia Nice, Jayne Malan, Eleanor Zimmerman Heward, Kathy Romney, John Barraclough, Noel Hilden, Dianne King, Carole Houtz, Lyle Moody, Kerry Marshall, Joyce Betita, Shari Southworth, Marla Jensen, and Barbara Dahl.

And finally, thanks to my nieces and nephews—Mary, Robyn, Emily, Rachel, Rebekah, Sarah, Derek, Jared Joseph, Cameron, and Daniel—who experimented and worked with me at "Camp Dian" to create many of the wonders of girls camp that you'll find in this book.

CHAPTER I

PLANNING

The first ingredient of a successful girls camp is a good plan. Planning requires decisions related to time, destination, budget, theme, activities, organization, equipment, clothing, and food. This chapter is designed to give you basic information and helpful ideas about everything you need to do before heading to camp. Use it to make preliminary decisions.

TIME

The first thing to decide when planning a trip, of course, is how long you will spend at camp. Will your camp be one day,

1

several days, a week? The duration of your camp will determine your needs and what you must take for a successful trip.

DESTINATION

Your destination will determine how soon and how carefully you must plan your camp. For example, you may need to plan far enough in advance to obtain a permit or make a reservation. Gather as much pertinent information as possible about your selected destination so you can accurately plan and prepare. A visit to your destination ahead of time, if practical, will greatly assist you in determining conditions and making plans. For a camp location where shopping is impossible, plan to make careful purchases beforehand for all your needs. For areas where potable water is unavailable, plan on bringing your own drinking water.

BUDGET

It is imperative that you determine your budget before making camp plans. Your budget should cover transportation costs, meals, and activities for the duration of the camp. Get your request in early so you know what you have to work with and can allocate funds appropriately.

THEME

Many camps are designed around a theme. You can set a theme for individual activities, campfire programs, or the entire camp itself. If a theme has not been assigned, you may want to consider the following list of possible camp themes:

- Feed My Sheep
- Armies of Helaman
- Daughters of a King
- Faith in Every Footstep
- Sailing Home

- A Star is Born
- A Royal Family
- Planting Seeds of Strength
- Noah's Ark
- Pioneers
- My Legacy of Faith
- Stand as a Witness
- Happiness Is . . .
- I'll Be Your Friend
- I Enjoy Being a Young Woman

ACTIVITIES

You will need to develop a schedule of each day's activities and then plan equipment, clothing, and meals around those activities. A short afternoon hike, for example, will probably leave you plenty of time to fix a big dinner upon your return. For an all-day hike, on the other hand, plan a hearty breakfast, a simple sack lunch, and a snack for energy. If you intend to return to camp late, plan to prepare a quick, easy meal upon your return.

Camp certification gives you several activities around which to plan your camp. If you teach outdoor certification skills with fun and enthusiasm, the young women will have a great time during camp and receive their certification after camp.

ORGANIZATION

Organization will help your camp run smoothly. A detailed plan that involves all campers will make the camp experience more satisfying for everyone. Your plan will vary depending on activities and numbers of participants, but if campers are involved beforehand in organizing the trip, they will know what to bring to camp and what their duties are once they arrive.

Youth Camp Leaders

The camp director's job is to coordinate all activities and responsibilities, but all campers should participate in making the camp successful. Young women who are sixteen and older are considered Youth Camp Leaders (YCLs); use them as such. By the time young women turn sixteen, they are usually camp veterans who have been trained in camp skills and are enthusiastic, eager to succeed, and love camp.

An effective camp program provides an opportunity for these young women to hone their leadership skills as they help plan, organize, and execute camp activities. It is important that YCLs be involved in the total process. The more they're involved, the more they will grow.

Select a strong adult leader to work with the YCLs. This leader, along with other camp leaders, should select a Youth Camp Leader as head of the YCLs. Look for a young woman with proven leadership skills. She will be your pivot person as you organize camp events and leadership experiences for the YCLs.

Put YCLs in charge of such activities as:
- The camp theme
- The opening ceremony
- Campfire programs
- Scripture study
- The flag ceremony
- Secret Sisters
- First-year certification
- Second-year certification
- Third-year certification
- Fourth-year certification

Leader Responsibilities

Some assignments may be combined, depending on the number of leaders available. To help with organization and to define responsibilities, consider the following designated roles:

Equipment specialist: This leader arranges for and supervises the packing of camp equipment, sees that it is properly cared for at camp, and returns each piece to its proper place (and owner).

Food specialist: Acting as a chef and menu planner, this person coordinates with the camp director the planning of meals. She also needs to coordinate with the equipment specialist to arrange for necessary kitchen equipment. At camp, she makes assignments related to meal preparation, serving, and cleanup.

Campfire specialist: Although everyone will join in singing and choosing songs, this person should coordinate the program for each night's campfire, make program assignments, and serve as song leader.

Fire specialist: This person should oversee the building and tending of all fires as well as arrange to bring firewood or supervise the gathering of firewood at your campsite (if permitted). She should bring a shovel and bucket and make sure that all fires are built and extinguished according to proper safety standards.

Certification specialist: Each age group has different certification requirements. One person may oversee the certification of all age groups, or a specialist may be assigned to each age group, depending on the number of young women at camp.

Activity specialists: These specialists are in charge of gathering necessary equipment and planning, organizing, and directing activities and games.

Crafts specialist: The crafts specialist plans craft projects and organizes supplies and materials.

Hiking specialist: This person acquires maps of the area, checks young women in and out of the camping area on hikes (in groups of at least two persons), and organizes group hikes.

First-aid specialist: The camp "doctor" or "nurse" arranges first-aid supplies, cares for minor injuries, and is prepared (with a cell phone, for example) to call for help in case of a major emergency.

Camp history specialist: This person keeps a camp record, takes camp pictures, encourages the young women to write in their journals, and gathers suggestions for future camps.

Conservation specialist: The conservation specialist sees that the group establishes conservation standards and keeps them.

Shopping specialist: Each branch, ward, or stake should be responsible for developing its own menus and doing its own grocery shopping unless the stake has been put in charge of food. If possible, one person should compile the shopping list, organize the shopping, and keep track of expenditures.

Transportation specialist: This person obtains a map to the destination and arranges for the transportation of young women, leaders, and equipment to and from camp.

Campsite assistant: The campsite assistant should help the camp director organize camp setup (including tent assignments) and cleanup. If necessary, this assignment can be divided into two jobs, with one person helping with camp setup and one person helping with camp cleanup.

For the specialists to plan and carry out their jobs, leaders need to provide them with as much detail as possible. Specialists need a schedule and budget, and they should be made aware of rules and restrictions. The following pages will help leaders plan and implement these suggestions.

The leaders, of course, can do camp-related tasks more quickly and easily than the young women, but the young women need opportunities to learn and participate. Involving them as much as possible in camp activities is the key to helping them grow and have a full and meaningful experience. For this reason, I designed the following technique for delegating meal-preparation responsibilities. This technique works well with groups of six or more that will cook at least three meals. Using this technique, leaders coordinate and assign responsibilities and oversee the young women as they perform tasks and learn from experience.

Divide the campers into three small groups. Each group will have one of the following duties: (1) fire building, (2) cooking, or (3) cleaning up. The three groups will switch duties at each meal. If fire building is not needed, you may want to divide cleanup duties between two groups—one before the meal and one after. See the following checklist for a detailed list of job responsibilities.

Checklist for Meal Responsibilities

Fire Builders Cooking with Open Fires

- Gather wood for the fire. (Make sure wood gathering is permitted; some parks and national forests restrict the practice.) If firewood is not available, bring plenty from home.
- Have a shovel and bucket of water on hand to extinguish and control fires.
- Consult with the cooks and build the type of fire they request. If coals are required, start the fire early enough to allow for ample coals.
- Assign someone to take care of the fire as long as it is needed.
- Extinguish the fire.

Fire Builders Cooking with Gas Stoves

- Review safety procedures before lighting camp stoves.
- Because setting up camp stoves takes little effort, this person should assist the cooks in preparing the meal.
- Clean stoves after use.

Cooks

- Determine the type of fire you need and ask the fire builders to prepare it.
- Determine how much time you need to cook each menu item so you can prepare accordingly.
- Organize the cooking area to prepare the meal.
- Soap the outside of all kettles to be used in an open fire.
- Set out needed condiments or utensils.
- Prepare and cook food.

Cleanup (before meal)

- Clear off, clean, and set tables. If practical, prepare a centerpiece using items from nature.
- Place garbage bags in garbage cans, or hang garbage bags nearby.
- Prepare an area for dishwashing.
- Before sitting down to eat, begin heating dishwater.

Cleanup (after meal)

- Put away leftover food.
- Wash dishes and cooking utensils.
- Clean up food-preparation areas.
- Make sure the camp area is clean and neat.

PLANNING MEETINGS

It's important that stake and ward Young Women presidencies, advisers, camp specialists, Youth Camp Leaders, and young women coordinate plans to ensure that everyone knows what is expected of them. Regularly scheduled meetings are essential for making plans, updating everyone involved, and tracking camp preparations. These meetings should also be used to determine what additional help and resources may be needed.

First meeting (six to twelve months before camp)
- Determine date, location, and budget.
- Review list of advisers, parents, priesthood leaders, and other adults who could serve as camp specialists and leaders.
- Discuss expectations and guidelines.

Second meeting (six months before camp)
- Determine whom to call as camp specialists and leaders. Key people such as the equipment and food specialists should be called as soon as possible to give them adequate time to plan and prepare. Other leaders should be called at least five months before camp.
- Begin planning activities and preparing daily schedules.

Third meeting (four months before camp)
- Train adult specialists and YCLs.
- Continue preparing daily schedules and activities.
- Plan an orientation meeting at which campers will receive packing lists, permission forms, and any other needed information to help them prepare for camp. Also announce a deadline for these forms to be turned in.

Fourth meeting (two months before camp)
- Review list of campers and status of required permission forms.
- Review daily master schedule.
- Review progress of specialist assignments.

Fifth meeting (one month before camp)
Review final plans from each specialist and distribute:
- A transportation plan and a map to the destination, prepared by the transportation specialist.
- A diagram of the campsite and list of tent assignments to the campsite assistant.

- A list of participation assignments for nightly campfire programs to the campfire specialist.
- A daily master schedule to all leaders.
- A list of campers to all leaders.

Sixth meeting (shortly after camp)
- Evaluate your girls camp.
- Thank and congratulate all who contributed.
- Gather suggestions for next year's camp.

PRE-CAMP PRACTICE

Practice is the key to gaining experience and having a successful camp because it takes away fear and uncertainty. If you or the young women need more experience, plan some practice runs at home or church. You can improvise a fire pit or a camp grill by using one of the techniques discussed below. Plan a menu and create a practice activity. Leaders can also practice with family and friends. Nothing takes the place of experience.

Unique Improvised Grills

If you don't own a barbecue and are planning a practice run, a day at the beach, a picnic, or an overnighter in your backyard, consider turning a wagon or wheelbarrow into a grill.

Use the wagon or wheelbarrow to tote your supplies to your site. Adapting them for grilling is as easy as filling the base with

Figure 1–1.
Wheelbarrow grill.

10

Figure 1–2.
Wagon grill.

six inches of gravel, sand, or dirt to insulate the bottom from heat. Cover the dirt with extra-heavy-duty aluminum foil to prevent coals from sinking into the dirt and to ensure that air will circulate. Make a pyramid of charcoal briquettes in the center of the foil. Pour lighter fluid over the charcoal and light. Drape a pair of oven mitts over the wagon tongue or wheelbarrow handles so they'll be close by when needed.

Arrange bricks around the outside edge, adapting them for a grill or rotisserie. If you simply want to do stick cooking, omit the bricks. The most efficient height for grilling is three to four inches above the coals.

MASTER PLANNING CHART

Dates of Trip _____   Destination _____

Contact Person _____   Telephone _____

Theme _____   Budget _____

Young Women Attending	Certification Year	Permission Received
_____	_____	_____
_____	_____	_____
_____	_____	_____
_____	_____	_____
_____	_____	_____
_____	_____	_____
_____	_____	_____
_____	_____	_____
_____	_____	_____
_____	_____	_____
_____	_____	_____
_____	_____	_____
_____	_____	_____

* This chart and the forms that follow are available at
www.campingwithdian.com/forms.htm

DAILY MASTER SCHEDULE

Include details for each day, such as mealtimes, activities,
crafts, hikes, certification training, and campfires.

Day 1
(Allow time for travel and camp setup)

7 A.M. ——————————   3 P.M. ——————————

8 A.M. ——————————   4 P.M. ——————————

9 A.M. ——————————   5 P.M. ——————————

10 A.M. ——————————   6 P.M. ——————————

11 A.M. ——————————   7 P.M. ——————————

12 noon ——————————   8 P.M. ——————————

1 P.M. ——————————   9 P.M. ——————————

2 P.M. ——————————   10 P.M. ——————————

Day 2

7 A.M. ——————————   3 P.M. ——————————

8 A.M. ——————————   4 P.M. ——————————

9 A.M. ——————————   5 P.M. ——————————

10 A.M. ——————————   6 P.M. ——————————

11 A.M. ——————————   7 P.M. ——————————

12 noon ——————————   8 P.M. ——————————

1 P.M. ——————————   9 P.M. ——————————

2 P.M. ——————————   10 P.M. ——————————

Day 3

7 A.M. ——————————   3 P.M. ——————————

8 A.M. ——————————   4 P.M. ——————————

9 A.M. ——————————   5 P.M. ——————————

10 A.M. ——————————   6 P.M. ——————————

11 A.M. ——————————   7 P.M. ——————————

12 noon ——————————   8 P.M. ——————————

1 P.M. ——————————   9 P.M. ——————————

2 P.M. ——————————   10 P.M. ——————————

Day 4
(Allow time for camp cleanup and travel)

7 A.M. ——————————   3 P.M. ——————————

8 A.M. ——————————   4 P.M. ——————————

9 A.M. ——————————   5 P.M. ——————————

10 A.M. ——————————   6 P.M. ——————————

11 A.M. ——————————   7 P.M. ——————————

12 noon ——————————   8 P.M. ——————————

1 P.M. ——————————   9 P.M. ——————————

2 P.M. ——————————   10 P.M. ——————————

CAMP SPECIALISTS

Duty	Name/Telephone	Responsibilities
Camp director	————————	Coordinates all activities and responsibilities.
Equipment specialist	————————	Obtains, packs, and returns all needed equipment.
Food specialist	————————	Creates menus, packs food, directs groups in meal preparation and cleanup.
Campfire specialist	————————	Coordinates campfire programs and selects and leads songs.
Fire specialist	————————	Obtains firewood and helps fire builders build, tend, and extinguish fires.
Certification specialist	————————	Oversees certification of all age groups.
Activity specialist	————————	Plans and organizes all games and activities.
Crafts specialist	————————	Creates craft projects and organizes supplies.
Hiking specialist	————————	Acquires maps of the area, monitors and organizes hikes.
First-aid specialist	————————	Provides first-aid supplies and care for first-aid problems.
Camp history specialist	————————	Keeps camp record, takes pictures, encourages young women to write journals.
Conservation specialist	————————	Sets up and monitors good conservation standards.
Shopping specialist	————————	Organizes shopping and monitors expenditures.
Transportation specialist	————————	Arranges transportation to and from camp.
Campsite assistant	————————	Helps camp director organize camp setup and cleanup.

MEAL DUTY CHART

Day	Meal	Fire Builders	Cooks	Cleanup Before	Cleanup After
1	Breakfast				
1	Lunch				
1	Dinner				
2	Breakfast				
2	Lunch				
2	Dinner				
3	Breakfast				
3	Lunch				
3	Dinner				
4	Breakfast				
4	Lunch				
4	Dinner				

PARENTAL OR GUARDIAN PERMISSION
AND MEDICAL RELEASE

Activity _____ Date _____

Ward _____ Stake _____

Participant _____ Birth date and year _____

Address _____ Home phone _____

Parent or Guardian _____ Work phone _____

Other emergency contact _____ Phone _____

Doctor _____ Phone _____

Last tetanus booster _____

Drug allergies _____

Other allergies _____

Special diet _____

Surgery or serious illness in the past year _____ explain on back

Physical conditions that limit activities _____ explain on back

Chronic or recurring illness _____ explain on back

Medication _____

AUTHORIZATION FOR TREATMENT

I give permission for my daughter to participate in the activity listed above. In case of medical emergency, I understand that every effort will be made to contact parents or guardians. In the event that I cannot be reached, I hereby authorize the adult leaders supervising this activitiy to administer emergency treatment to the above-named participant for any accident or illness and to act in my stead in approving necessary medical care. This authorization shall cover this activity and travel to and from this activity.

Signature of parent or guardian _____ Date _____

Family insurance carrier _____ Policy No. _____

CHAPTER 2

EQUIPMENT

The variety of equipment made for campers is so vast that no one can afford to have everything on hand that a group of young women and their leaders might use at camp. You would need a fortune to buy all the great items available, a transportation fleet to carry them, and a computer system to keep them organized.

On the other hand, if you pool camping equipment, you'll likely have all the gear you need. Ask your young women leaders, parents of young women, and ward scout leaders what camping supplies they have. Then determine what you lack, and improvise using household articles. You'll be surprised what you can create with a few basic tools and a little know-how. If pooling and improvising doesn't work, you can rent camping equipment from stores that sell sporting goods and from colleges that rent outdoor supplies.

Consider the safety and accessibility of your camping area and the length of your stay before planning what equipment to take. Obviously, you can take more equipment if you're driving rather than hiking to your camp. Dutch ovens are great, but you wouldn't want to pack one very far.

COOKING EQUIPMENT

The length of your stay and the accessibility of your campsite will dictate what cooking equipment to take. Selecting the right items is the key to preparing delicious meals in the out-doors. An easy way to decide what to bring is to plan your meals first; then determine what you need to prepare those meals.

Here are some suggestions to help you improvise:

- A No. 10 can makes a versatile utensil that can be used to cook in, to mix foods in, and to serve from, and it can be disposed of without a second thought. Recycle a potato flake can, a food storage can, or other similar cans for use outdoors.
- If you need to take water, you can carry it in plastic reclosable bags placed inside cans for leak-proof trans-portation. Before mixing food, line cans with plastic reclosable bags. Afterward, discard bags.
- To reduce the number of dirty pans you generate, take along large oven cooking bags for lining pots. Discard bags after use.
- A smooth-sided tin can may be used as a rolling pin. (Do not use glass containers.)
- A tuna fish can makes a good cookie or biscuit cutter when both ends are removed.
- Cut out the sides and bottom of a plastic bleach bottle to create a homemade scoop.
- Heavy-duty aluminum foil can be shaped into a serving bowl. It can also be turned into a frying pan by wrapping it around a wire coat hanger shaped into a rectangle. You can deepen a shallow pan by building up its sides with foil.
- Plastic reclosable bags are handy for mixing food. Simply combine all ingredients, push most of the air out, seal, and squeeze until ingredients are mixed. To coat food before cooking, combine flour and seasonings in a bag, drop in pieces of meat or chicken, and toss. Bags are also good for preparing muffin and cake mixes. Before empty-ing a mix into a bag, cut the instructions from the mix box

and tape them to the bag's outside. When you're ready to mix, add the liquid ingredients, squeeze the air out of the bag, seal it, and mix by squeezing with your hands.

- A heavy-duty reclosable bag can be used to hold cookies, crackers, or nuts for crushing.
- A Frisbee can double as a serving tray for paper plates. Give each young woman a different-colored Frisbee lined with a stack of paper plates to last the entire camp. At the end of a meal, they peel off and discard the top plate. If you're serving a meal with more than one course, they can peel off a plate after each course.
- Control insect problems by using an embroidery-hoop lid. Fasten a piece of plastic wrap between the two rings of an embroidery hoop as if it were a piece of fabric to be stitched. Place the hoop over a plate or bowl, and you will prevent flies and gnats from invading your dish. You'll also prevent your food from drying out.
- Organize tools and utensils using a hanging shoe or lingerie organizer with see-through pockets. The pockets are perfect for holding paper plates, napkins, cups, and

cooking and eating utensils. This hanging equipment bag is storable in a kitchen or utility closet and transfers easily to an outdoor hook or tree branch. If a storm threatens your outing, your equipment stays dry within the compartments of the bag. Should you choose to move indoors or to another site, you can pack your cooking equipment in just minutes.

Figure 2–1. *Embroidery hoops and plastic wrap keep insects off food.*

20

FIRE EQUIPMENT

Shovel and water bucket. If you're planning on having an open fire, keep a shovel and water bucket within ten feet in case of a fire emergency. If you plan on cutting wood, bring a saw; if you plan on splitting wood, bring an ax. Leaders should demonstrate proper use and care of these tools, which young women are allowed to use only under careful supervision. Axes must be covered at all times when not in use, and two-headed axes are not permitted.

Heat-proof gloves. Heat-proof gloves are helpful for setting pans and aluminum-foil dinners on, and for removing them from, fire and coals. They're also useful in handling hot Dutch oven lids. Use heat-proof gloves any way you would use a hot pad. If you can't find heat-proof gloves, which are available from welding suppliers, use leather or other heavy gloves.

Charcoal briquettes. These small pillow-shaped coals offer a dependable source of steady heat for outdoor cooking.

Chimney starter. A chimney starter is an excellent tool for quickly and easily lighting charcoal briquettes.

Wood. Wood comes in two types: hardwood and softwood. Hardwoods, such as fruit and oak trees, are excellent for cooking. They provide hot coals that last long enough for cooking. Softwoods, such as aspen and pine, burn quickly and should be supplemented with charcoal briquettes for cooking. The number of meals you plan to cook over a fire and the type of wood available will determine how much wood you need. If you're planning evening campfires, you'll need even more wood. On average, an armload of hardwood burns for an hour.

TENTS

The types and sizes of tents on the market today are limitless. They range from small, lightweight tents to large tents with multiple compartments. Determine your needs based on terrain, climate, mode of transportation, and number of campers.

Type and Size

How many young women are coming to camp? Where will you store equipment in case of rain? Will you be hiking to your camp? When you know the answers to these questions, you can determine your shelter needs.

If you plan on driving all the way to camp, you can bring large, heavy, comfortable tents that have ample room for several people. (A large tent and poles may weigh fifty pounds or more.) If you plan on hiking to your campsite and carrying a tent in your backpack, you'll want to look for a small, durable, lightweight tent that is easily packed and assembled.

The following tent styles provide plenty of room for groups of varying size: umbrella, cabin, multicompartmental, and Springbar.

Umbrella tent. Umbrella tents offer more headroom than tepee tents, but their sloping walls limit the efficient use of floor space.

Figure 2–2. *Umbrella tent.*

Figure 2–3. *Cabin tent.*

Cabin (wall) tent. This basic A-structure tent has vertical walls but its guylines require time and effort to set up.

Multicompartmental tent. As its name signifies, this tent has multiple compartments that can be turned into a variety of rooms: kitchen, bedrooms, and so forth.

Springbar tent. This tent, though large and heavy, is easily assembled and provides plenty of room, including ample headroom.

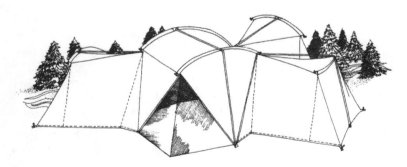

Figure 2–4. *Multicompartmental tent.*

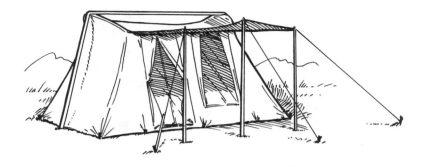

Figure 2–5. *Springbar tent.*

Materials and Construction

Most tents are constructed from synthetics or canvas. Nylon, used in many tents on the market, is popular because it is lightweight and durable. Nylon resists fading and weather wear despite prolonged exposure to the elements. Tent floors are often made of urethane-coated nylon, and most tent roofs feature a separate polyester rain fly. Some tents are made of lightweight canvas, which is durable but heavier than synthetic fibers. Make sure canvas tents are thoroughly dry before storing.

In a good tent, its stress points are reinforced with a double seam, and its corners are reinforced with an extra layer of fabric. The seams run in the direction of the support, which is usually vertical, not horizontal. A horizontal seam is located somewhere above the floor of the tent where the sidewalls attach. This seam prevents water from entering the tent through the seams and running onto the floor. Most tent poles are made from lightweight aluminum, and stakes are made from aluminum or plastic.

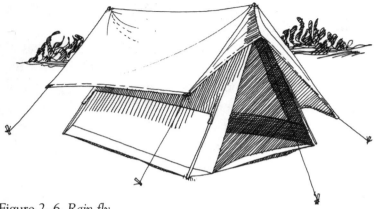

Figure 2–6. *Rain fly.*

Ease of Assembly

Setting up a large tent requires a little teamwork, but even big tents that use several poles for support are remarkably simple to assemble. If you're assembling a tent for the first time, consider a dry run in your backyard, or have the young women help you set up the tent as part of an activity night. This will allow you to resolve any problems and determine whether you have all the tent poles and stakes. Learning how to put up a tent in familiar surroundings under a sunny sky is far easier than doing so in the dark of night during a rainstorm.

Tent Accessories

To be caught without necessary accessories when you're attempting to pitch a tent guarantees a frustrating experience—especially if it's raining. Give a little forethought to each piece of equipment to avoid disasters at your campsite.

Guylines. Guylines are ropes connected to the tent and tied to surrounding trees, logs, or rocks for added tent support. Bring along plenty of rope just in case you need to make guylines.

Stakes. Extra stakes always come in handy. Tents that tend to be like box kites when the wind blows need extra stakes in order to remain secure. If the ground is too soft to stake, tie guy-lines to logs or rocks.

Poles. Most poles are made from aluminum and are strong and lightweight. They are also easy to replace should you lose one or irreparably bend one. Bring along some extras just in case.

Shovel and hammer. A shovel comes in handy when removing rocks or leveling out a spot for a tent. Keep a hammer on hand for pounding stakes into the ground and for straightening bent stakes or poles.

Ground cloth. You and your sleeping bag will stay drier if you pitch your tent on a ground cloth.

Tent Care

Keep it dry. Be aware that nylon mildews if it remains wet. When breaking camp, let the sun dry your tent thoroughly. If you don't have time or it's raining while you're breaking camp, roll up and stow your tent, but unfold it and dry it out once you reach home. Then store it in a dry place. Keep your tent in its carrying case off the floor so that it is not exposed to condensation and moisture.

Keep it hole free. Before you pitch your tent, remove rocks and twigs from your tent site. Be wary of pitching your tent under a tree full of dead branches that could fall on your tent and puncture it, and keep rocks and sharp objects away from your tent once it is set up. Punctures can turn into big holes and rips. Before you know it, you'll need a new tent. When you pack your tent, place the stakes and poles in separate stuff sacks to avoid damaging the tent.

Keep it clean. To prolong the use of your tent, get into the habit of keeping the inside and outside clean. A ground cloth made of either coated nylon or plastic will keep grime and dirt off the bottom of the tent, and a whisk broom will help you sweep out the twigs and dirt. If your tent comes home muddy, set it up in your backyard, spray it off with a hose, and let it dry before putting it away.

GENERAL CAMPING EQUIPMENT LIST

The following is a checklist of general camping and cooking equipment:

- ❑ Aluminum foil
- ❑ Ax, hatchet, saw
- ❑ Briquettes
- ❑ Buckets
- ❑ Bulletin board (portable)
- ❑ Camp stove and fuel
- ❑ Can openers
- ❑ Clothesline and clothespins
- ❑ Cooking pots
- ❑ Cutting boards
- ❑ Dishcloths
- ❑ Dishpans
- ❑ Dish soap
- ❑ Dish scrubbers
- ❑ Duct tape
- ❑ Dutch ovens
- ❑ Fireproof gloves
- ❑ Firewood
- ❑ Food coolers
- ❑ Frying pans
- ❑ Garbage bags
- ❑ Ground cloths
- ❑ Kettle (large, for water)
- ❑ Knives
- ❑ Lantern (extra mantles and fuel)
- ❑ Markers
- ❑ Matches

- ❑ Measuring cups
- ❑ Mixing bowls
- ❑ Mixing spoons
- ❑ Newspaper (for starting fires)
- ❑ Pancake turner
- ❑ Paper towels
- ❑ Plastic bags (reclosable)
- ❑ Potato peelers
- ❑ Pot holders
- ❑ Rope
- ❑ Scissors
- ❑ Shovel
- ❑ Silverware
- ❑ Spatulas
- ❑ String
- ❑ Tablecloths
- ❑ Tape
- ❑ Tarps
- ❑ Tents
- ❑ Thumbtacks
- ❑ Tin snips
- ❑ Tongs
- ❑ Twine
- ❑ Water coolers
- ❑ Whetstone
- ❑ Whistle
- ❑ Wire

PERSONAL EQUIPMENT

It's hard to escape housekeeping and personal grooming concerns, especially while camping or traveling, but you can make these easy and fun if you put your creative talents to work.

Clothing

Climate and trip length dictate the amount and type of clothing to take. Plan clothing to give protection and warmth while allowing freedom of movement for activities. Encourage campers to take only the essentials, keeping in mind planned activities.

Shoes. Shoes are especially important if you plan to hike. Young women should bring a sturdy, comfortable pair that provides support and protection. Sneakers provide neither. New shoes should be broken in at home, not during a hike.

Socks. Lightweight socks are good to wear around camp, but for hiking, wool socks are best because they absorb moisture and cushion the feet. Wearing two pairs of socks during a hike—a light pair under a heavier pair—will help prevent blisters.

Pants. Every young woman should have at least one pair of sturdy long pants. Long pants provide protection from branches, sharp rocks, sunburn, insect bites, and cooking burns. Tight-fitting pants should be avoided because they restrain movement, and short pants are not recommended, especially on hikes, because they expose the wearer to scratches, bug bites, and sunburn. Some stakes prohibit shorts altogether.

Shirts. Long sleeves provide protection against sunburn, insects, and evening coolness. Young women should bring at least one long-sleeved shirt, even during the hottest part of summer.

Hat. A hat offers protection from the sun and will hold in body heat during cool weather. If you plan on taking a midday hike, a hat is essential.

Coat. A warm coat is a welcome relief from night and early morning chill, especially if you're camping in the mountains.

Insect repellent. Insects are attracted by perfume, hair spray, cosmetics, soap, lotion, and body oils. Repellent with 5–10 percent deet, the substance that keeps bugs away, lasts up to two hours. Repellent with 15 percent deet content will last up to four hours; 25 percent deet, up to six hours; 100 percent deet, up to ten hours.

RAIN EQUIPMENT

Water-repellent jackets, ponchos, and ground cloths are a must, particularly in mountainous areas that are prone to rain. Ground cloths can be used to protect camping gear, cover woodpiles, or build shelters. A large garbage bag or square of plastic sheeting can be used as an improvised poncho. To turn a large plastic bag into a poncho, cut a hole in the bottom of the bag for your head, and cut holes on both sides of the bag for your arms. To turn a square of plastic sheeting into a poncho, simply cut a hole out of the center for your head. Be careful not to cut the hole too big.

SLEEPING EQUIPMENT

A good sleeping bag ensures a good night's sleep so you can enjoy the next day's activities. The types of sleeping bags available vary from down- or fiber-filled bags made for the extreme cold of winter to lightweight backpacking bags made for warm summer nights.

Types of Sleeping Bags

Rectangular bag. A rectangular bag is the same size at the bottom as at the top. The zipper on this bag zips across the bottom and up the side, allowing the bag to be opened. It can be used as a quilt, or it can be zipped to another bag and used as a double bag, provided the zippers on the two bags match. A rectangular bag gives you enough room to move your legs. One disadvantage of the rectangular bag is that its greater space requires more body energy to warm it on cold nights.

Tapered bag (semirectangular). The tapered bag is similar to the rectangular bag, but it follows the shape of the body. It is wider at the shoulders and narrower at the feet. It restricts movement in the feet area but is lighter and easier to warm up.

Mummy bag. A mummy bag is shaped like a cocoon. It further restricts movement, but its construction requires less body heat to warm up the bag, and its drawstring helps you keep the warmth inside the bag. Mummy bags offer the most protection for extreme conditions.

Bag construction. Shells for sleeping bags range from cotton and light canvas to synthetic materials like nylon. Some bags come with genuine down filling, but most family bags are filled with synthetic fibers. Depending on a bag's filling, it may feature a quilt stitch, a perimeter stitch, or interior baffles, used in down bags to reduce fill movement. Lining is usually flannel cotton or nylon.

The price of a sleeping bag varies with the performance of the bag, the quality of the filling, and its temperature rating. Bags are generally filled with Hollofil or Polarguard polyester, which varies in thickness and compressibility. These synthetics do not absorb water, so bags containing them dry quickly and are usually machine washable. Liteloft, a more efficient synthetic, imitates down and offers the greatest warmth-to-weight ratio of the synthetics. Protect the loft of your high-quality sleeping bags by storing them on clothes hangers rather than in stuff bags.

Packing List

The following list (found at www.campingwithdian.com/forms.htm) can be adapted for specific conditions and activities. Quantities should be determined by length of stay.

Clothing

- ❑ Coat
- ❑ Poncho, raincoat, or water-repellent jacket
- ❑ Sweater or sweatshirt

- ❑ Shirts
- ❑ Pants (two pair)
- ❑ Shorts (knee-length)
- ❑ Bathing suit (one-piece)
- ❑ Gloves (for warmth and work)
- ❑ Shoes (two pair—one for hiking)
- ❑ Sandals
- ❑ Socks (several pair)
- ❑ Underclothing
- ❑ Pajamas and slippers
- ❑ Hat
- ❑ Plastic bags (to keep clothes dry and to store dirty clothes)

Personal Items

- ❑ Comb and brush
- ❑ Toilet paper
- ❑ Deodorant
- ❑ Sunscreen
- ❑ Feminine hygiene products
- ❑ Insect repellent (with high deet content)
- ❑ Toothbrush and toothpaste
- ❑ Dental floss
- ❑ Lip balm
- ❑ Towel and washcloth
- ❑ Soap and shampoo
- ❑ Medications
- ❑ Mirror

Sleeping Equipment

- ❑ Ground cloth
- ❑ Pillow
- ❑ Air mattress or sleeping pad
- ❑ Sleeping bag
- ❑ Extra blanket

Miscellaneous

- ❏ Flashlight and extra batteries
- ❏ Daypack
- ❏ Mess kit
- ❏ Silverware kit
- ❏ Canteen or water bottle
- ❏ Stainless steel cup
- ❏ Watch
- ❏ Camera and film
- ❏ First-aid kit
- ❏ Pocketknife (if needed for certification)
- ❏ Compass
- ❏ Sunglasses
- ❏ Scriptures
- ❏ Journal
- ❏ Musical instrument
- ❏ Camp manual
- ❏ Notebook and pencil

CHAPTER 3

SETTING UP CAMP

Like building a home, planning and setting up an outdoor living area can be a creative and meaningful experience. But a campsite is temporary, so you must plan to remove every trace of your stay at the end of your camp. Remember these mottos:

- Meet your needs without changing the beauties of nature.
- Leave an area better than you found it.
- Leave nothing but tracks; take nothing but pictures.

CAMPSITE SELECTION

If you plan to use out-of-the-way camping areas, whether public or private, obtain permission from landowners or government agencies. If you haven't already selected a campsite, use the following criteria in making your choice.

Suitability

Does the site have suitable areas for preparing food, cooking, and sleeping? Does it have toilet facilities? Does it have potable water? Whenever possible, investigate campsites ahead of time, and arrive early enough to assess facilities and set up camp before it gets dark.

Protection

Your first consideration should be the safety of individual campers and the protection of the natural beauty found at your campsite. Place tents and camping equipment on high ground in case of rain and flash floods. Use existing vegetation to provide protection and privacy.

Whenever possible, find a campsite sheltered from the prevailing direction of the wind. Wind tearing at the flaps of your tent can create an unpleasant experience, making it hard to sleep and intensifying the cold.

One of the most tormenting experiences for campers is being attacked by insects. Your tent should be as airtight as possible, and shelters should have insect-proof netting. The following suggestions may help you avoid insects:

Avoid damp areas. Insects breed in moist habitats. The drier your campsite, the freer from insects you will be.

Search for a breeze. Insects don't like breezes. If you can find a site with a constant movement of air, your chances of avoiding an insect onslaught are better.

Provisions

Is your campsite near water and dry wood? If not, you will need to make arrangements to bring them with you. It is usually a good idea to bring wood as well as charcoal briquettes.

Cautions

If you are in bear country, don't take chances, and don't believe anyone who assures you, "The bears around here are tame."

Put food out of reach. Store food outside the tent, and place it high enough that a bear can't reach it and far enough away from camp that a bear won't associate it with your camp. Storing it in a car is also safe.

Eat outside. If possible, refrain from eating in tents, where the odor of food will linger and invite a bear's curiosity. Food odor also clings to clothing, so bring along several changes. Also, avoid perfume.

Do not feed bears. Once fed, a bear will come searching for more food. If you're asleep and unable to grant his desires, he may become dangerous.

Sleeping Area

If you learn to pitch a tent successfully, you will have won half the battle of trying to enjoy the outdoors. The following suggestions may help.

Protect your tents from puncture by removing rocks and twigs from the area and keeping rocks and sharp objects away after the tents are pitched. To temporarily repair rips or punctures while camping, use a piece of duct tape. Don't forget to do permanent repairs once you return home.

Set up your tent on a smooth, flat area free of bumps, roots, and immovable rocks. If no level spot is available, pitch your tent so that your head is uphill. If possible, choose a spot that affords natural protection from the elements—trees, bushes, and so forth—but that will receive the morning sun.

Pitch tents on high ground so that if it rains, water will run away from your campsite. Avoid the environmentally destructive practice of digging trenches around tents. Avoid swampy areas where mosquitoes congregate, and stay clear of rock walls, rotten trees, rockslides, or dead, overhanging branches. Falling tree limbs and rocks can give campers a dangerous wake-up call.

Pitch your tents upwind and well away from your campfire so that you can avoid blowing sparks that could result in fire or injury. Avoid burning dry pine boughs or weeds that could shoot sparks toward your tents.

Kitchen

In the outdoor kitchen, as with any kitchen, everything will run more smoothly if you are organized and if you designate specific areas for specific duties. The kitchen might include storage areas for staple and refrigerated foods, an equipment area, a food preparation and cooking area, an eating area, and a cleanup area.

Storage of Staple Foods

One of the best places to organize a food supply is in a tent. Organize food items according to particular needs for each meal (breakfasts,

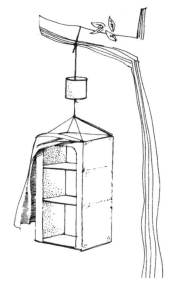

Figure 3–1. *Box for storing staple foods.*

lunches, dinners) or by category, such as spices and seasonings, canned goods, and mixed ingredients. Organization should be clear enough so that cooks can easily find what they need.

Food requires protection from animals and insects. Plastic or sturdy cardboard storage containers with tight-fitting lids work well, as do boxes or gunnysacks hung from tree limbs. If rodents are a problem and you lack adequate storage containers, place food in a bag (or box), tie the bag closed with a rope, tie a knot in the rope above the bag, make a hole in the bottom of a can, slip the can above the knot, and hang the bag from a tree (see Figure 3–1). This will protect your food from large animals and will prevent rodents from crawling down the rope into the stored food.

Storage of Perishable Foods

One of three types of outdoor refrigeration should suit your needs for storing perishable foods: streams, burlap coolers, or commercial coolers.

Figure 3–2. *Creek refrigerator.*

Streams. Look for a shady, shallow spot at the edge of a creek. Place perishables in a laundry basket, burlap bag, wooden crate, or five-gallon plastic bucket, and then lower it into the cool water. Anchor the container by placing rocks in and around it and by tying it to a tree or a large rock at the edge of the stream.

Burlap coolers. A hanging portable cooler can be made from burlap, thin plywood, and rope. Cut plywood into two-foot squares (or the size desired). Drill holes the width of a small rope in each corner and thread rope through the corner holes. Tie knots the distance desired between the shelves. Hang the shelves by the rope ends from a tree in a cool, shady place, and cover them with burlap. The burlap should be stapled or attached to all edges of the shelves except in the front, which should be overlapped so that the burlap can be

Figure 3–3. *Hanging portable burlap cooler.*

separated for access. Extend part of the burlap above the top of the cooler sufficiently to be immersed in a pan of water that sits on the top shelf. If the burlap is saturated with water to begin with and the top edges of the burlap are kept in the pan of water, it will stay wet by absorption and cool by evaporation. (This does not work well in humid climates.)

Commercial coolers. A commercial cooler is handy and effective. Water, juice, or soft drinks in plastic bottles can be frozen and placed in coolers to keep them cool. (Freezing liquid in glass bottles can cause them to burst. When freezing liquid or any other item in a container, leave room at the top for the liquid to expand when it freezes.) Milk can also be frozen to help keep coolers cool, but the freezing process separates the protein and may change the flavor somewhat. Shake the milk well before using. Before leaving for camp, freeze any meat you plan to use two to three days into your camping trip.

You can use commercial ice, "blue ice," or dry ice in coolers. Always wear gloves when handling dry ice, and pack it in newspaper. Do not put dry ice in an enclosed container; it must be stored so that it can release carbon dioxide.

Storage Hints

- If you plan to store cheese for a long period of time, wrap it in cheesecloth that has been dipped in vinegar. This will reduce mold.
- Place a piece of apple, lemon, or orange inside a covered container of brown sugar to keep the sugar soft.
- Prevent salt from lumping in humid climates by placing rice in the saltshaker. The rice will absorb the moisture and keep the salt dry.
- Place sugar, powdered sugar, and salt and pepper in large shakers with lids. Before traveling, unscrew the lids, place plastic wrap over the shakers, and screw the lids over the

wrap. This will prevent the contents from spilling. In camp, remove the wrap. Then label or color code the shakers to indicate their contents.

- Store unripe bananas or avocados in brown paper bags. Gases given off by the fruit will speed ripening.
- Measure and prepackage foods before leaving home. Prepare ahead of time the necessary quantities of muffin and biscuit mix, blending all ingredients except liquid and eggs. Make sure you tape recipes to the outside of containers so you know how much liquid and eggs to add.
- Store dry bread crumbs in plastic containers or plastic bags. Use bread crumbs to augment meat and egg dishes; use pastry crumbs or cake crumbs as toppings for puddings and desserts.
- Store eggs in plastic egg holders, or break them into a quart jar or plastic container with a tight seal. They will

Figure 3–4. Plastic egg holder.

pour out one at a time. Use them within four days, and keep them in the cooler at all times. If you store eggs with the large end up, they will stay fresh longer. To check for freshness, place an egg in water. If it sits at the bottom of the pan, it's fresh. If it rises and floats, it has lost moisture and freshness. To avoid salmonella, serve eggs completely cooked with no runny yolks or whites.

- Place bread in a shoebox or plastic container to keep it from being smashed.
- Protect items packaged in glass jars by placing them in plastic containers during travel.
- Buy butter or margarine in plastic containers for convenient use.

40

Food Preparation Area

Many campsites have picnic tables that can be used for preparing food. If not, bring a portable table, use a wooden equipment box, or spread a tarp on a flat rock or on the ground. Keep the area organized and clean as you work. Return all supplies to their storage areas following food preparation, and rinse all dishes before the food dries and becomes difficult to remove.

Cooking Area

An essential part of camping is planning and establishing the cooking area. Your cooking area should have pots, pans, grills, Dutch ovens, serving utensils, cooking utensils, hot pads, gloves, cooking oil, seasonings, and everything else you need in close proximity. A plastic storage box or fishing tackle box works great for organizing utensils and spices.

Many established campsites have built-in fire areas. If you are camping in an area with no established fire area, get permission to prepare one. See chapter 5 for a complete course in fire building.

Eating Area

If a table is not available, select a shady spot and spread out a large piece of plastic or ground cloth. To add a special touch, prepare a centerpiece for the eating area. In the evening, consider enjoying the warmth and informality of eating around the campfire. Use a large log for seating, or construct a log bench following these steps:

- Saw two 5- to 8-inch-diameter logs about two feet long.
- Cut a groove in the top of each of these logs so that another log (five to six feet long) can rest in the grooves without rolling.
- Place the small wedged logs under each end of the long log you will use as a seat.

41

Figure 3–5. *Log bench.*

Cleanup Area

The cleanup area is important for health and sanitation. Efficient cleanup procedures save time and prevent unnecessary work. The following suggestions may be helpful.

- Soap the outsides of all pans with liquid detergent or soap lather before using them on an open fire. The soap will stay between the pan and the black buildup, making the buildup easy to remove.
- When making desserts containing lots of sugar, line your cooking containers with heavy-duty aluminum foil to make cleanup easier.
- Use paper towels to wipe off dishes and remove grease from pans before washing them.
- Begin heating dishwater before beginning to eat. Gallon cans work well for heating water.
- If a pan is hard to clean, put water in it and bring the water to boil to soften hard-to-remove food particles.
- Use salt or sand to clean off warm cast-iron grills.

Washing dishes. Soapy hot water is important for getting dishes clean. If your water is not clean enough to drink, add a little liquid bleach to your dishwater or boil your rinse water and dip dishes into it to kill germs.

Figure 3–6.
Soaping pots and pans used over an open fire makes cleaning easy.

A simple dishwashing station can be made by constructing a wooden table with two round holes cut in the top. Make each hole just smaller than the lip of a round plastic garbage pail. The two plastic garbage pails should fit inside the holes but be held up by their outside lips. One container can hold soapy water, while the other can hold rinse water.

After rinsing dishes, sterilize them by placing them in a cloth or net bag and then immersing the bag in boiling water. A drawstring should be pulled around the top of the bag so the bag can be closed before it's dropped into the water. Afterward, the

Figure 3–7. *Hot water tank.*

bag may be tied to a rope that has been stretched between two trees or tied to the limb of a tree so that the dishes may dry.

Hot water container. Galvanized metal buckets make good hot water containers. Five-gallon fire-resistant metal cans are available in Salt Lake City at Utah Barrel and Supply, 370 West 900 South, 84101. They can be placed on the edge of a fire for constant hot water. A ladle may be placed in the container for campers to retrieve water as needed. You can easily turn a No. 10 can into a billycan (see page 69).

Equipment Area

Every piece of camping equipment should be stored in its proper place. As the saying goes, "A place for everything and everything in its place." Here are some good general rules to follow in using and storing camping equipment:

Exercise caution. Establish a cutting or sawing area that is always supervised by an adult. Keep people a safe distance away while wood is being cut or sawed. Take precautions and use axes, saws, and knives safely.

Be careful with equipment that uses kerosene or other liquid fuels, and follow directions carefully. Portable heaters may be used indoors or in tents only if they have been designed for such use. Even then, do not use heaters while sleeping, keep all flammable materials at least two feet away from them, and create an opening to the outside of at least six inches square to allow for fresh air.

Proper use. Use the proper tool for the proper job. Don't let young women abuse knives by stabbing them into the ground, and require that they use a hammer rather than the side of an ax to pound in tent pegs.

Proper repair. Do not use damaged equipment. You may break it beyond repair. Keep cutting equipment sharp and in good repair. Repair broken equipment before putting it away so it will be ready the next time you need it.

Proper Storage

Always place saws, axes, hatchets, and knives in their proper storage places when not using them. To prevent rust, cover cutting blades with sheaths, and wrap metal parts in heavy canvas. Store equipment off the ground and protect it from moisture. Be careful not to

Figure 3–8. *Equipment bag.*

store gas- or oil-filled equipment where it can create a safety hazard or lead to contamination. After camp, clean all equipment before you store it.

Hanging equipment bag. A hanging vinyl bag with see-through sections is effective for storing such things as paper plates, napkins, and utensils. Items can be categorized and placed in each see-through section. The sections can be stitched or partially stitched at one end to keep equipment from sliding out. The vinyl covering keeps contents dry when it rains.

Plastic boxes. An efficient way to transport and store camping equipment is to use plastic boxes. Boxes make packing efficient and help keep your campsite organized. Label boxes as follows:

- Non-food items: aluminum foil, plastic wrap, paper towels, matches, toilet tissue, napkins, plastic bags, garbage bags, paper cups and plates, plastic utensils, tablecloth.

- Staples: syrup, soup mixes, hot cocoa mix, salt, pepper, and other spices.

- Cooking supplies: hot pads, steel wool pads, knives, spatulas, tongs, mixing spoons, measuring cups and spoons, can opener, silverware, cutting board, dish towels, collapsible water jug, frying pans, pots, and dish soap.
- Tools: flashlight, lantern, saw, hatchet, shovel, fireproof gloves, pliers, screwdriver, batteries, rope, insect repellent, duct tape, rope or twine, and first-aid kit.

Lunch or tackle box. An old lunch box or fishing tackle box can easily be turned into a handy storage box for your cooking paraphernalia. Use it to store your spices and sauces, pot holders, utensils, and other items you might need. Both lunch and tackle boxes come in various sizes, so look around to find one that suits your needs.

Plastic cleaning container. These durable containers have handles and are divided into compartments. They can be used to easily organize cooking utensils and spices.

Carpenter's apron. If you would rather have all your cooking necessities at your fingertips, buy a carpenter's apron. The large front pockets provide plenty of space for all the tools you need for outdoor cooking.

Cooking shirt. The cooking shirt is a combination apron/pot holder. It has a breast pocket to hold various items and is a great way to cover up and keep your clothes clean. It's also a great way to recycle two old shirts. To make a cooking shirt, you need a long-sleeved sweatshirt and a long-sleeved button-type shirt made of a durable material like denim or flannel.

1. Cut off the sleeves of the button-type shirt a few inches below the elbow.

2. Cut off the sleeves of the sweatshirt above the elbow, almost to the armpit.

3. Place together the cut edges of the shirtsleeves and the sweatshirt sleeves, right sides together, and pin at the seam. (If both shirts are not the same distance around, see tip below.)

4. Pin right sides together. Sew a five-eighths-inch seam joining both shirts.

You now have an extra-long sweatshirt sleeve at the end of your button-type shirt. Push the sweatshirt sleeves down when cooking, draping them over your hands to lift hot pans and to protect yourself from heat. The cooking shirt is also ideal for keeping your hands warm or roasting marshmallows on a cool evening around a campfire.

Tip: Sometimes the circumference of the sweatshirt sleeves is larger than the shirtsleeves. In this case, sew a new seam from the cuff to the cut edge of the sweatshirt, making it the same distance around, or gather by stitching two basting seams around the cut edge of the sweatshirt sleeve at five-eighths inch and one-quarter inch and easing them together. Pin at each one-half inch and then at one-quarter inch, and sew a permanent seam at five-eighths inch. Old shirts and sweatshirts can be found at thrift stores.

Figure 3–9. *Cooking shirt.*

Bathroom Area

Keeping clean can be a real challenge when camping, but hygiene is extremely important. Several fun ideas in this section will simplify the daily routine for young women. First of all, whenever bathing or washing clothes in the outdoors, campers should use biodegradable soap and do all washing (including brushing teeth) far enough away from lakes and streams to protect them from contamination.

Grooming apron. If you have trouble finding a convenient place in camp to keep and organize items for brushing your teeth and combing your hair, make a handy apron for personal items. Making grooming aprons is a fun sewing project for young women prior to camp.

To make a grooming apron, take a bath towel, fold up the lower edge about five inches, and sew pockets to hold such items as toothpaste, soap, razor, comb, mirror, and washcloth. Sew a casing about two inches above the pockets and thread a drawstring through it, making it long enough to tie around your waist. The excess material at the top of the towel becomes a flap to keep items from falling out of their pockets and can serve as a towel for drying your hands and face.

Waterspout. Poke a small nail hole in the front of a plastic bleach bottle near the bottom. Fill the bottle with water. When you're ready to wash your hands, loosen the bottle's lid. The pressure from the top will force a small stream of water from the spout. To create a larger stream of water, poke a hole with a golf tee. Tie the tee to the bottle's handle so it can

Figure 3–10.
Grooming apron.

Figure 3–11. *Waterspout.*

48

be used as a stopper. Attach a rope to the handle and tie the bottle to a tree limb. Place a bar of biodegradable soap in a nylon stocking, and hang it from the bottle's handle. Paint a face on the bottle with the mouth over the spout area and you'll smile every time you use it.

Outdoor shower. If your young women are hesitant about camping because they're afraid they'll have to do without a daily shower, they need fear no more. An outdoor shower is quick and simple to assemble, and it works beautifully. To make a shower room, you'll need an umbrella (without a sharp point), two shower curtains, and some rope. Open the umbrella and turn it upside down. Then tie one end of the rope to the umbrella handle. Throw the other end over a tree limb and loosely tie it to the tree trunk so the umbrella is at eye level. Hook the curtain holes onto the prongs of the umbrella, raise the umbrella so that the bottom of the shower curtain is off the ground, and tie the rope securely to the tree.

For your showerhead, purchase a new insecticide sprayer and mark the outside "CAMPING ONLY." Never use anything that once contained chemicals. For your hot water heater, buy a large black can or paint a can black. Another option is a commercial Sun Shower (made by Basic Designs), which features a flat plastic bag (clear on one side and black on the other) and a sprinkler head shut-off valve.

Leave your water in the sun during the day for a heated afternoon shower. The shower room is also a good place to change clothes.

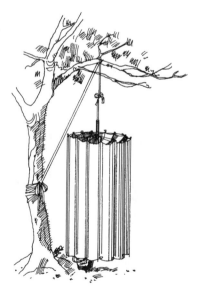

Figure 3–12. *Outdoor shower.*

49

Bring along a rubber doormat (the kind with holes) to stand on, and your feet will stay clean.

Nighttime bathroom tissue holder. This easy tissue paper and flashlight holder will help your young women find their way in the dark and keep their tissue dry. To make it, remove the cardboard tube from inside the center of a roll of bathroom tissue. Pull the paper out of the center of the roll. Place the roll and a flashlight inside a plastic reclosable bag. Pull enough tissue from the center of the roll so that it hangs outside the corner of the bag. Close the bag to the corner. Use the flashlight to find your way to and from the latrine.

Figure 3–13. *Nighttime tissue holder.*

Sanitation

Campers and hikers have an obligation, for their own protection and for the protection of others, to properly dispose of waste. It is best to use available facilities wherever they exist, but in the wild you may not have access to such luxuries. In that case, pack out whatever you pack in, including food, trash, hygiene products, and toilet paper.

Urine poses few problems for campers and the environment other than odor. It evaporates quickly and contains few organisms that can transmit disease. Solid human waste is another matter, and extreme care should be taken for its proper disposal. Feces left on or near the ground surface, especially anywhere near water, can pollute an astonishingly large area. Even when the amount of waste is small and buried, bacteria carrying disease can travel a good distance through the surrounding soil.

Before setting out on a camping or backpacking trip, always determine the disposal method recommended for the area you'll be visiting. The best alternative for solid waste disposal—one endorsed by the National Park Service and environmentalists, and the only alternative in many high-use areas and waterways—is to pack it out. Empty ammunition cans and double or triple plastic bags are frequently recommended as suitable containers. Another good choice is a portable potty made from a standard five-gallon plastic bucket lined with a heavy

Figure 3–14. *Portable potty.*

plastic bag and topped with a specially designed snap-on toilet lid. The Deluxe Water/Sanitation Kit (available from Emergency Essentials, 1–800–999–1863; www.beprepared.com) is a five-gallon water storage and portable toilet in one compact unit.

Latrines. Where digging is permitted, a latrine is probably the best solution if you plan to camp in one spot for several days. Pick a site at least two hundred feet away from campsites, waterways (whether water is running or not), and established trails. Avoid selecting a spot that another group might choose as a camp or picnic site.

Prepare your latrine immediately after arriving at camp by digging a narrow trench about a foot and a half deep and a foot wide. Preserve the sod. If you need more capacity, make your trench longer, not deeper. If you dig below the topsoil into inert-looking earth, microorganisms cannot properly decompose the organic material. If you dig a shallow hole, waste could wash away with the first rainstorm, often into lakes and streams, or become an attraction for flies and other insects.

After each use, throw in fresh soil or ashes. With large groups, you should also use lime (available at a garden store) to counteract odors, repel flies, and hasten decomposition. Fill the hole and restore the sod before leaving the campsite.

A single-use "cat hole" is recommended only for individuals or small groups. Select sites using the same guidelines given for a latrine, and scatter the holes to eliminate concentration in one place. Dig a small hole six to eight inches deep. After use, fill the hole by tamping dirt into it, and restore the area to its natural appearance.

Toilet paper may be the most objectionable aspect of the human waste problem because it lasts a lot longer than fecal material. If buried or left, it deteriorates slowly, leaving telltale signs for months, even years. Use biodegradable ("green") toilet paper, or put toilet paper into a small plastic bag to burn on a fire not being used for cooking.

Do not bury trash, including tampons, sanitary napkins, or diapers, which decompose even more slowly than toilet paper and whose odors will attract animals. If you are bringing a baby to camp, dispose of diaper waste as you would any other fecal waste, and *never* wash diapers in streams or lakes.

LEAVE YOUR CAMPSITE CLEAN

We all like to arrive at a clean campsite. Good manners demand that we leave our camp clean for the next campers.

If you are in an undeveloped area where fire building is allowed and you have built your own fire area, restore it to its natural state. Bury your ashes, and scatter the stones used to ring your fire pit.

Any shelves or poles lashed to trees should be taken down. Take all lashing twine with you. All cans, aluminum foil, and organic garbage should be disposed of in a garbage can or packed out.

Before leaving camp, young women should go over every inch of the campsite to make sure all garbage has been picked up and properly disposed of. Have young women form a human line, hands outstretched and touching the person next to them, and move through camp to make sure all paper and trash has been picked up. This may require several sweeps moving in different directions.

QUAD POD

One of the best ways to keep your campsite clean and organized is to set up a quad pod. A quad pod is especially useful in the food-preparation, cooking, eating, and cleanup areas. Sticks can be lashed across the top of the quad pod to hold utensils, paper towels, and other items. Cross-sticks can be taken out of the quad pod so it can accommodate a plastic pan for washing dishes. For instructions on making a quad pod, go to www.campingwithdian.com/lashing.htm.

Figure 3–15.
Quad pod.

CHAPTER 4

SAFETY

Making camp safe for everyone should be a top priority for young women and their leaders. Being exposed to the elements in the outdoors creates many opportunities for accidents or injuries. But with good training and proper programs, you can make camp a safe place for all.

FIRST AID

Knowledge of first aid is essential for safe camping. Young women should learn first aid before and during camp as part of fulfilling their certification requirements. Being prepared with the right knowledge and materials in emergencies can save the day, or even a life.

FIRST-AID KITS

Each girls camp should have a first-aid kit, each ward or group should have a first-aid kit, and each young woman should have a first-aid kit. One of the best ways to get a quality first-aid kit is through the Red Cross. The Red Cross offers individual, family, and group first-aid kits as well as pamphlets on first aid and other safety issues. Check your local Red Cross or the Red Cross website (www.redcross.org) for availability. A list of items to be included in each young woman's first-aid kit is found in the *Young Women Camp Manual*.

Figure 4–1. *Weather creates nature's delights as well as its dangers.*

DANGERS

Campers may encounter a number of dangers in the out-doors, including the following:

Weather. Weather creates many of nature's delights and many of its dangers. One of those dangers is excessive exposure to the sun. Since outdoor experiences mean spending more time outdoors, the dangers of exposure are increased. High altitudes and reflection from water, sand, or snow can increase the danger of sunburn, even on cloudy days. All campers should bring and wear sunblock at all times on all exposed skin. Sunblock is rated according to its strength. Young women should use sunblock with a rating of at least SPF 30.

If your camp includes swimming or boating activities, those participating should apply and reapply sunscreen. When hiking or spending extended periods of time in the sun, campers should wear hats and long-sleeved shirts. They should also bring and drink plenty of water and stay alert for signs of heat exhaustion. Keep aloe vera gel handy for young women who may burn despite precautions.

Know the climate and dangers in your camping area. On a long hike, you might need to be prepared for rain and lightning, even on days that begin clear and sunny. Packing a trash bag for an improvised rain poncho could mean the difference between a fun hike and hypothermia.

Lightning storms are a real danger. In some areas, storms can build quickly and move fast. Campers who find themselves in a lightning storm should get off ridges of high mountains, stay away from bodies of water, and avoid taking refuge under trees, especially lone trees that could easily become targets of lightning strikes.

Campers should also be aware of storms in areas prone to flash floods. Check the weather report, and avoid areas that could be prone to flash flooding.

Insects and animals. Each young woman should bring her own insect repellent to camp. Insect repellent containing deet gives the best and longest-lasting protection. The more deet it contains, the more effective it will be. Some insect repellents are combined with sunscreen for a double-duty product. When insects are biting, long pants and long-sleeved shirts are necessities.

Young women should know what animals and insects they will find at camp and and how to deal with them. Skunks, poisonous snakes, ticks, and even deer, squirrels, and chipmunks can be trouble if an inexperienced camper meets them unprepared. See chapter 3 for cautions about camping in bear country.

Tools. Some camping tools may be unfamiliar to the young women. Certain tools can be dangerous in inexperienced or careless hands. Be sure your young women understand how to properly use knives, axes, and saws. Giving a badge or bead to those who know and promise to keep safety rules is a good way to ensure sharp tools are used safely.

Set aside an area for woodcutting by taping or fencing it off to restrict access. This area should be far enough away from camp to allow space for flying wood chips or slipping tools.

Camp trails. Develop safe paths between tents and other areas of the camp. Pay special attention to paths that will be traveled after dark. Take care that downed trees, big rocks, exposed roots, or other tripping hazards are cleared from paths or are well marked.

Instruct campers not to run downhill or roughhouse through the camp. Be sure every camper has her own flashlight with a spare bulb and batteries.

Your camp should have well-defined boundaries, and young women should stay within the camp boundaries unless accompanied by an adult.

Pranks. Pranks are generally done in fun, but they can destroy a good camping experience. In some cases, they have hurt people emotionally and physically. Leaders should enforce a no-pranks policy or stipulate that pranks must be service oriented and cleared in advance.

CHAPTER 5

FIRE BUILDING AND CAMP STOVES

Fire building is a skill that all campers must learn in order to complete their certification requirements. While there's no substitute for the cozy warmth of a campfire, we must be increasingly sensitive to the environment. Fire building requires thoughtful concern and care. One campfire ring provides cheery comfort and a delightful social atmosphere; a hundred campfires blight the landscape.

Most county, state, and federal campsites have fire rings to encourage and contain campfires. These rings allow you to enjoy a campfire and cause no damage to the environment. Use them when they're available.

Before deciding on a campsite, find out about the area's fire regulations and recommendations. While fire building might be okay in some areas in the spring and fall, it is often prohibited during dry summer months. It is always wise to go prepared to cook with charcoal briquettes or a camp stove. I prefer teaching campers to use briquettes because they simulate coals from a fire. Many of the suggestions for campfire cooking in this book can be applied equally well to charcoal briquettes and camp stove cooking.

FIRE-BUILDING GUIDELINES

If you're not camping in an officially designated camp-ground, the following information will provide you with guide-lines for doing your part to preserve the environment. Fire building is acceptable when:

- You bring your own wood or you know there is an abun-dance of wood on the ground.
- A fire site already exists and is in a good location.
- You take appropriate safety precautions, especially if you have to select and make your own campfire site.

To build a fire, select a spot at least fifteen feet from trees, bushes, and fallen trees. Fires built over roots are dangerous because the fire can follow ground-level roots back to trees or bushes. Never build a fire directly under branches or near dry grass or weeds. Always be aware of wind speed and direction. Sparks can travel great distances, and smoke can annoy your neighbors. Look for spots that may have already been used for a fire, and circle your fire area with large rocks.

Keep your fire small. Big fires produce too much heat and make it difficult to control the cooking temperature. Most cook-ing is best done on hot coals or charcoal briquettes rather than on direct flames. If you're going to burn wood from the camp-site, take care not to burn large downed branches that may be home to small animals.

Basic fire-building equipment includes a shovel, fire grate, ax, and water bucket. Keep your shovel nearby and your water bucket filled in case your fire gets out of control. Never leave your fire unattended, and before leaving your campsite, put out your fire by drowning it with water. Stir the ashes so that every ember is out. Whenever possible, haul out your ashes and restore the area to its natural state.

Firewood

To start a fire and keep it burning, you need tinder, kindling, and fuel.

Tinder. Tinder is anything smaller than your finger that will burn and help you start a fire. Some examples of tinder are dry grass or leaves, small twigs, dry pine needles, fine wood shavings, bark, or strips of paper.

Good tinder can be prepared at home in a cardboard egg carton. Fill the pockets of the carton with cotton balls or lint (saved from your dryer). Place the egg carton on a section of newspaper. Melt paraffin or old candles in a double boiler and pour the wax into each lint pocket. Break off a pocket of the egg carton every time you need a fire starter. The pocket will burn ten to fifteen minutes.

Figure 5–1. *Egg carton fire starter.*

Kindling. Kindling is wood that ranges in diameter from the size of your little finger to the size of your wrist. Use kindling to stoke the fire until it is large enough to burn larger pieces of wood.

Fuel. Fuel is wood larger in diameter than your wrist. Use it to sustain your fire.

Building an A-Frame

An A-frame around a tinder tepee is the best way to start your fire. It is also the perfect way to use your tinder, ensuring that your fire starts successfully. Follow these simple steps to make an A-frame.

• In the center of a fire circle, make a triangular A-frame

60

with three sticks approximately one-inch in diameter and a foot long. Place one end of each stick on the ground and the other end so that it overlaps another stick.

- In the center of the A-frame, make a tepee with tinder, starting with fine materials and gradually adding larger pieces. Place some kindling around the tepee.
- Over the A-frame, lay the type of fire structure you desire. Light the tinder while it's still accessible, even if the fire structure is not entirely laid.
- Lay the fire so that air can circulate among the materials. Without enough air, the fire won't burn. You can fan the smoldering fire with a paper plate. Be careful not to get too close to the flame.

Types of Fires

Fires are generally named for the manner in which the wood is stacked.

Tepee. The tepee fire is a basic fire used to begin other fires. Lay the A-frame and tinder tepee. Then build another tepee around your tinder tepee with kindling and fuel. The high flames of this fire are good for one-pot cooking and for a reflector oven (see chapter 6).

Log cabin fire. To get a good bed of coals, build a log cabin fire by forming a basic A-frame and a tinder tepee. Then place overlapping logs around the tepee as if you were building a miniature log cabin. Gradually lay the logs nearer the center as you build the cabin, giving it the appearance of a pyramid. Coals will form quickly as the fire burns.

Crisscross fire. For a large, deep bed of coals for roasting or Dutch oven cooking, prepare a crisscross fire. After forming an A-frame, tinder tepee, and kindling tepee, light your fire. Then place logs on the fire in layers, one layer crossing the other. Leave a little space between each log for air to circulate.

Figure 5–2. *Basic A-frame with tepee kindling.*

Figure 5–3. *Tepee fire.*

Figure 5–4. *Log cabin fire.*

Figure 5–5. *Crisscross fire.*

Figure 5–6. *Star fire.*

Figure 5–7. *Keyhole fire configuration.*

Star fire. This fire is sometimes called the lazy man's fire because as the logs on this fire burn down, they are simply pushed farther into the flames. This fire is useful for preparing one-pot meals. Use the A-frame, a tinder tepee, and a kindling tepee to begin the fire. Then feed long logs into the fire as needed. A star fire is also a good way to burn wood for an evening campfire.

Keyhole fire. The keyhole is the most efficient design for both a campfire and a cooking fire because it supplies constant fresh coals to keep your cooking area hot. Build a keyhole configuration using rocks or bricks (Figure 5–7). Then build a log cabin fire or a crisscross fire in the larger, upper keyhole area. As coals become ready and as you need them, move them with a shovel from the upper area into the lower area. The lower keyhole provides a stable place for a grill.

Methods of Starting a Fire

A fire can be started in many ways. Some of the more primitive ways are fun to learn and can be used in times of emergency.

Matches. The most common method of starting a fire is with matches. You can buy waterproof matches or you can waterproof them yourself by dipping them in paraffin or fingernail polish. After dipping the matches, place them in the grooves of a piece of corrugated cardboard and allow them to dry. Keep the matches in a waterproof container.

Figure 5–8. *Matches dipped in paraffin or fingernail polish.*

Flashlight batteries and steel wool. A rather dramatic method of starting a fire is to conduct electricity from two flashlight batteries through steel wool. This is an excellent way to start a fire when the wind is blowing. Cut or tear 00 or a finer-grade steel wool roll into a half-inch strip, which will lengthen out to a strip about seven inches long. Place the batteries (any size) on top

Figure 5–9. *Flashlight batteries and steel wool.*

of each other, making sure both are in an upright position as if they were in a flashlight. Hold one end of the strip of steel wool against the bottom of the lower battery. Rub the other end of the steel wool across the top of the top battery. After the steel wool sparks, place it next to the tinder and blow on it softly. Always pack steel wool and batteries in separate containers.

Flint and steel. A meat cutter's steel (a piece of metal used to sharpen knives), a steel knife blade, or a file struck against stone will cause sparks. The sparks will create a thin wisp of smoke if they come in contact with dry tinder. When the smoke appears, blow gently with short puffs of air until the tinder bursts into flame. Fine tinder or charred cloth will facilitate ignition. A spark in fine steel wool will also work.

Magnifying glass. A magnifying glass placed in the direct sunlight so that a fine point of light is focused on dry tinder will cause the tinder to smoke and eventually break into flame.

Extinguishing a Fire

Knowing how to extinguish a fire properly is as important as knowing how to start one. Use the following steps to extinguish a fire.

1. First, break up the fire with a shovel or stick and spread out the coals.

2. Sprinkle water over the coals. Don't suddenly pour a large amount of water on a hot fire. The steam might burn you or any bystanders.

3. Stir the fire with the shovel or stick, drenching it with water until the coals are cool enough to touch.

4. If large logs have been burning, make sure any fire inside the log is out. Remember, a fire is not out until the coals are cool enough to touch.

Most accidental fires can be put out quickly by eliminating the oxygen that feeds them. For instance, a shovel of dirt thrown on a grease fire will extinguish the flame. If your clothing catches fire, roll on the ground to put it out. Extinguish a spark on the ground by stomping on it with your shoe. Take sensible precautions to prevent accidental fires. In a strong wind, it's best not to light a fire.

In many camping areas, open fires are illegal because of the fire hazard. Increasingly, campers are forced to use other methods to cook their food.

CAMP STOVE COOKING

For personal safety reasons and with respect for the environment, most recipes in this book call for a camp stove, Dutch oven, or grill.

When cars became more affordable at the end of World War I, many families took advantage of their newfound mobility to explore the great American outdoors. Fold-up camp stoves soon became traveling companions in car trunks and were found in vacation cabins, camping trailers, and hunting lodges. Their popularity has increased ever since.

To select a stove for outdoor use, consider variables such as what food and how much of it you'll be preparing, the availability of water, the distance you might have to carry supplies, climate conditions, terrain, and length of your outing.

Stoves are often classified by the type of fuel they burn. The most common fuels are propane, butane (cartridge or cans), and white gas. The following types of stoves are easy to carry and use for the camping recipes in this book.

Camp Stoves

Camp stoves come with one, two, or three burners. Stoves equipped with one burner weigh between one and two pounds. Two- and three-burner stoves weigh more but are ideal for cooking several items simultaneously. A three-burner stove is ideal for breakfast, for example, because you can place a griddle over two of the burners and use the third to heat beverages.

When purchasing your outdoor stove, consider one that comes with a windscreen attachment. This comes in handy when the wind suddenly picks up.

One-burner stove. The one-burner stove is excellent for general use except on a windy day. It has the advantage of a butane cartridge, which is easy to change. It's also lightweight and easily carried while camping.

Figure 5–10. *One-burner stove.*

Two-burner stove. A two-burner stove will burn for approximately two hours per fuel canister with both burners on high. The two-burner stove is inexpensive to operate and may be designed to consume both

Figure 5–11. *Two-burner stove with windshield.*

66

automotive unleaded gasoline as well as liquid fuel. It offers even heat distribution, deep flame ports on the sides for wind resistance, ease of lighting, adjustable flame, and a nickel-chrome-plated steel rod grill for easy cleaning.

Grill/griddle stove.
The grill stove is convenient for picnics and camp-
outs. Turn over the grill
and you have a griddle.
These stoves usually use
propane cylinders.

Figure 5–12. *Camp grill/griddle.*

Tin-can stove. One of the most innovative outdoor cook-ing methods, and an excellent indoor-cooking method in a fire-place, is the simple homemade tin-can stove, which can be used for frying, boiling, and toasting. It works best for one or two people because of its small size, and it's disposable. Just recycle after use.

To make a tin-can stove, cut out one end of a No. 10 can (102 ounce). With tin snips, cut two slits 3 inches high and 3½ inches apart on one side of the can at the open end. Bend the snipped section outward, forming a door. Using a punch-type can opener, punch two or three holes on the backside of the can near the top. These act as a chimney, allowing smoke to escape during cooking. Cut out the top end, and you can use a skillet on top of the can.

A tin-can stove is also great for making toast. Hold two slices of bread against opposite sides of a warm can, just behind the oven door.

Figure 5–13. *Tin-can stove.*

After you have held the bread for a moment, it will usually stick to the outside of the can. With a spatula or knife, pop the bread off when it has browned. The toast takes on the shape of the can, so toast only one side of the bread. A buddy burner (see below) is the main source of heat for a tin-can stove.

Buddy burner. To make a buddy burner, cut corrugated cardboard (across the corrugation so that the holes show) into strips the same width as the height of a tuna can. Roll strips tightly to fit inside the can. Heat wax in a double boiler and pour melted wax onto the cardboard, or set a piece of wax on the cardboard and light a match next to the wax. Continue adding wax near the flame until the buddy burner is filled. The cardboard serves as a wick, and the wax serves as the fuel, providing heat for the stove. To light it more easily, lay the can on its side so that the flame spreads across the cardboard. It will burn 1½–2 hours. To refuel, melt a new piece of wax in the burner while it is burning. When you're finished, let the wax harden before storing.

To control the amount of heat generated by a buddy burner, use a damper, which can be made of aluminum foil or from the lid of a tuna can. To make a damper, repeatedly fold an 18-by-15-inch piece of heavy-duty foil into three-inch sections until all the foil is folded. Bend the foil down as a handle to set over the tuna can. To make a damper out of a tuna can lid, punch holes in the top of the lid on each side. Next, take apart a clothes hanger

Figure 5–14. *Use wax, cardboard, and a tuna can to make a buddy burner.*

68

Figure 5–15. *Foil damper.*   Figure 5–16. *Can lid damper.*

and bend the ends so they are parallel. Wire the ends of the hanger to the can lid so the hanger serves as a handle. Bend the hanger so it props itself up while the buddy burner is burning. Move the damper to increase or decrease heat.

Billycan. A homemade oven, called a billycan, can be made easily from a No. 10 can and a clothes hanger or heavy wire. Cut one end out of the can and punch two small holes on opposite sides of that end for the handle. Bend back the metal from the punched holes to eliminate rough edges that

Figure 5–17. *Billycan.*

could cut someone. Straighten out a clothes hanger or wire and then curve it, securing the two ends to the holes punched through the can.

Fuels

The following paragraphs describe the characteristics and advantages of several common fuels. With all the fuel options available, you have many choices to meet cooking needs.

White gas. White gas is relatively inexpensive and easy to find at sporting goods and variety stores. Its main advantages are heat output and economy. It is sold in one-gallon cans. If you don't mind carrying a can to your outdoor destination, filling your liquid-fuel appliance, and occasionally pumping your appliance, white gas may be the right choice for you. Unlike butane and propane, this fuel burns hot even at subzero temperatures.

Figure 5–18. *White gas in a one-gallon can.*

Propane. Propane is the most popular camping fuel because it is so easy to use. Simply attach a propane fuel cylinder to your camp stove and begin cooking. Propane is heavier than other fuels, weighing two to three pounds per cylinder. It's reliable but generates less heat at subfreezing temperatures than white gas. Cold weather creates a pressure drop in the cylinder, which decreases propane fuel output. If you plan to camp for several days or weeks, you can cut fuel costs by using a large refillable propane tank.

Butane. This convenient, lightweight fuel is available at many

Figure 5–19. *Propane is available in small, convenient cylinders.*

sporting goods and restaurant supply stores. It may be the right choice if you plan on backpacking because butane and butane-fueled appliances weigh very little. Butane works best in fair weather. Subfreezing temperatures affect the pressure in the canister. Butane canisters are not recyclable.

Blended fuel. Propane/butane blended fuel performs well in cold temperatures and at high altitudes. It uses a liquid withdrawal system that ensures optimum performance when cold. It is available in recyclable aluminum canisters.

Unleaded gasoline. The main advantages of unleaded gas are availability and cost. Unleaded gasoline, which is about one-tenth the price of propane, is the least expensive of all fuels and is available at every gas station. In an emergency, it's possible to siphon

Figure 5–20. *Butane is ideal for backpackers.*

gas from your car and use it in a lantern or stove that runs on unleaded gasoline. Unleaded gas generally has a stronger odor than camping fuel.

White gas and unleaded gas are flammable and should be used and stored properly. Using unleaded gas in traditional gas stoves is not recommended except in emergency situations because it will lessen performance and reduce appliance life. Cooking with unleaded gas requires special care. Do not fill an appliance indoors or near a stove or open flame. Always clean up spills, and always follow the manufacturer's directions.

Tablets. Commercial fuel tablets, available at sporting goods stores, can be placed in a small stove and lit. These small tablets work well for warming canned food and other quick-cooking items. They may be used either with a tin-can stove or with a small commercial stove made expressly for their use. If a stove is not available, place stones closely around the tablets to serve as support for small cooking pots and cans.

Canned heat. Canned heat can be used for cooking or warming food in cans. You can purchase stoves that are made to use canned heat, such as Sterno.

Paraffin. Make your own canned heat by rolling narrow strips of corrugated cardboard into a tuna can and filling the can with melted paraffin. (See "buddy burner" on page 68.) This is a good activity for young women at camp, particularly if you plan to use the tin-can stove cooking method.

Charcoal briquettes. Charcoal is one of the best options when open fires are not permitted or when gathering wood is illegal. Use them for grilling meat and cooking foil dinners, and for Dutch oven, spit, and stick cooking. Charcoal briquettes can be placed on the ground or on a piece of heavy-duty foil, especially if the ground is wet.

Remember these rules when using charcoal briquettes:

1. Never start briquettes with homemade lighter fluid or gasoline; they could explode.

2. Unless you're using a chimney starter or briquettes that light quickly, allow 35–45 minutes for the briquettes to produce coals for cooking.

3. Never burn briquettes in an enclosed area.

Chimney Starter

Crumple two full pages of newspaper into wadded balls and place them in the bottom section of the starter. Pile briquettes in the top above the newspapers. Light the newspapers. Fan a Frisbee or paper plate near the chimney's opening to increase air circulation and help the briquettes ignite. When briquettes glow red-hot, pour them into a fire bed and start cooking.

Starting Briquettes Over a Campfire

Briquettes can be added to wood fires to provide a better and larger bed of coals. Pour the briquettes onto the hot fire and allow them to heat for twenty to thirty minutes. An effective

Figure 5–21. *A chimney starter is an ideal way to quickly light charcoal briquettes.*

Figure 5–22. *Portable basket of hot briquettes.*

way to start charcoal briquettes over an open fire is to shape a screen (one-half- to three-quarter-inch mesh) into a bucket or bowl-shaped basket. Make a wire bale for lifting or carrying. Place the desired amount of charcoal briquettes into the basket and set it over an open fire. If the fire is hot, particularly if it has good flames, the charcoal will start quickly.

Commercial Starters

Commercially prepared charcoal lighter fluid and jellies come in handy. Follow directions so that you put the right amount of starter on the briquettes. Then close the starter container and move it away from sparks or flames before lighting the briquettes.

CHAPTER 6

COOKING METHODS

Preparing food outdoors can be especially satisfying. Wood-smoke flavoring, fresh air, cool mornings, warm campfires, and a healthy appetite, coupled with a little camp-cooking know-how, can lead to nutritious and delicious outdoor meals and a feeling of pride and satisfaction.

Besides encouraging a oneness with nature, outdoor cooking is a sensory experience that involves all five senses. You *watch* as hot dogs brown on a grill. You *hear* steaks sizzle. You *touch* the top of a Dutch oven cake to see if it *feels* done. You *smell* the aroma of slow-cooking stew. And, of course, you *taste* what you've cooked.

Cooking in the outdoors requires specific skills that can be developed using a few basic facts and guidelines. The carefully tested cooking methods and the proven recipes in this book will give you ideas on how to add interest and variety to your outdoor adventure. To plan your menu, consider preferences, methods of cooking, food costs, length of your camp, and number and ages of people who will be eating. One way to plan convenient, practical meals is to determine your activities first; then decide which meals would best accompany those activities.

This chapter will give you ideas on how to adapt familiar indoor cooking methods and principles in the outdoors. Refer to the following list for outdoor methods that can be used to

INDOOR COOKING METHODS DUPLICATED OUTDOORS

Bake	Cooking with dry heat	Tin-can stove Pit cooking Dutch oven Food inside of food Can oven Sand cooking Reflector oven
Barbecue	Cooking over direct heat and seasoning with barbecue sauce	Stick and spit Can barbecue
Boil	Cooking with water or moisture	Aluminum foil Liquid in paper cup Tin can, billycan Double boiler Dutch oven
Braise	Cooking slowly in a covered pan with sauce and a small amount of fat	Frying pan Dutch oven
Broil	Cooking with direct heat	Can barbecue Spit cooking Stick cooking
Fry	Cooking with a small amount of fat	Aluminum foil Dutch oven Frying pan Tin can stove
Roast	Cooking with dry heat	Tin can stove Reflector oven Dutch oven Pit cooking Can oven
Steam	Cooking with moist heat	Aluminum foil Dutch oven
Stew or slow roast	Cooking for a long time in a small amount of liquid	Dutch oven Pit cooking

duplicate familiar indoor results. Then look for instructions for a particular method of outdoor cooking to see what type of fire to build, equipment to purchase or make, foods to use, and step-by-step directions to follow. With the variety of easy food-preparation methods available to you, camp cooking should never become dull or routine.

High-Altitude Cooking

High-altitude cooking increases cooking time because liquids boil at approximately 2 degrees Fahrenheit less per 1,000 feet of altitude. In San Diego (sea level), water boils at 212 degrees. In Brighton, Utah (8,000 feet above sea level), water boils at 196 degrees (212 degrees minus 16 degrees). Food takes longer to cook the higher you go. For information on high-altitude cooking, consult a cookbook or the Internet.

Cooking Time

Learning to cook food in the outdoors without burning it is difficult at first but becomes easier with experience. In general, foods cooked outdoors should take about the same amount of time as foods cooked indoors. Don't be in a hurry. Foods cooked too fast may end up being burned, cooked on only one side, or partially raw. Cooking times may vary according to altitude, cooking temperature, and the amount of food being prepared.

Types of wood used for cooking. Cooking time varies according to the type of wood you use. Hardwood from broad-leafed trees makes hotter, longer-lasting coals, providing a more extended cooking time than the softwoods from needlelike, evergreen trees.

Concentration of coals. The amount and concentration, or thickness, of a coal bed also determines the length of cooking time. The more concentrated the coals, the shorter the cooking time.

How Hot Is the Fire?

To determine the amount of heat generated by a charcoal fire, hold your palm at cooking level and see how long you can keep it there:

2 seconds = high heat
3 seconds = medium-high heat
4 seconds = medium heat
5 seconds = medium-low heat
6 seconds = low heat

Adjust heat by raising or lowering your grilling rack and by concentrating or spreading out your coals.

Food is usually placed at an average height of three to four inches above the coals. If you plan to grill a thick cut of meat that needs to cook longer, move it farther away from the coals so that it will cook more slowly and thoroughly. Thinner cuts cook more quickly, so they can be placed closer to the coals. Don't crowd foods. Arrange food so that air can circulate evenly around each item.

Cooking without recipes. When preparing foods without following recipes, keep in mind these pointers:

1. When creating your own stew, always remember to brown onions and meat first. Then add water or broth and each vegetable according to how long it takes to cook—carrots and potatoes first, celery later.

2. When you boil pasta or rice, use two times as much water as dry ingredients. Bring the salted water to a boil first before adding pasta or rice. Add butter or oil to the boiling water so the water will not boil over and so that the pasta will not stick together. Cover your boiling pan and cook at a low, bubbling temperature. For precooked rice, simply add rice to boiling water and allow the water to return to a boil. Then remove the pan from the heat, cover it, and let it sit for about five minutes while the rice swells.

3. Use one-half teaspoon of salt for each pound of meat; one-half teaspoon of salt for each cup of flour; two tablespoons of flour for each cup of liquid (for medium thickening); one-quarter cup of powdered milk (instant) for each cup of water.

STICK COOKING

Almost everyone's first experience with outdoor cooking began with sticks to roast marshmallows or hot dogs. Thankfully, stick cooking has evolved to include simple and delicious meals suitable for the outdoors.

Equipment for stick cooking is readily available—roasting sticks, wooden dowels, clean pitchforks, commercial metal sticks, and, of course, actual sticks found anywhere outdoors. These can all be used over an open fire or bed of hot coals. Use your creativity and you'll discover the satisfaction of stick cooking for your favorite outdoor food.

Commercial metal sticks can be easily cleaned by putting them in coals to burn off drippings after use. Allow metal skewers to cool before reusing. Cooking sticks can be created from wooden dowels. Simply sharpen one end with a pencil sharpener or pocketknife. Before using bamboo or wooden skewers or sticks, it's a good idea to soak them in water for several hours so that they will not burn. Always cook over hot coals rather than in direct flames when using a stick.

Two Types of Stick Cooking

A limitless variety of foods can be cooked on a stick, including one of my favorite campfire treats: simple and delicious Roasted Cinnamon-Sugar Apple Pie on a Stick (see chapter 9). Stick cooking involves two methods: end-of-the-stick cooking and kabob or whole-stick cooking.

End-of-the-stick cooking. Place food on the end of the stick and rotate it so food cooks evenly. Hot dogs and marshmallows are the most common items cooked this way. Remember, the larger the item, the farther it should be held away from the coals.

Whole-stick (kabob) cooking. Slide cubes of meat and pieces of fruits and vegetables along the entire stick or skewer. Visually attractive and taste-tempting kabobs can be prepared as a main dish, salad, or dessert—or all

Figure 6–1. *Hot dogs, apples, and bread can be cooked to perfection on a stick.*

three at once. A tasty and creative way to serve kabobs is to arrange a selection of different foods on serving plates and let each young woman assemble her own kabob. Because kabobs often include an assortment of tastes, textures, and colors, they are a popular and versatile menu choice.

For evenly cooked, flavorful, and attractive kabobs, select foods requiring about the same cooking time. If a variety of cooking times is needed, kabob foods will be both overdone and underdone. If you want to use cherry tomatoes or banana chunks that require less cooking, add these toward the end of the cooking time. Use fairly uni-

Figure 6–2. *Select foods to skewer that require similar cooking times.*

form sizes for even cooking, and be aware that small food pieces may pop or split if the skewer is too large for the food.

Thread food pieces directly through the center to prevent food from drooping and falling into the coals. Using two skewers adds additional stability to your kabob. Place kabobs on a grill. If the coals beneath are too hot, food that is well cooked on the outside may be undercooked in the center.

For meat kabobs, use tender cubes of meat cut to the same size. Meat requires moisture and fat to become tender; stick cooking is a dry-heat method. To use less-tender cuts of meat, marinate for several hours before cooking. An acid-base marinade (such as orange or lemon juice, vinegar, or tomato juice) helps to tenderize meat and increase flavor.

Figure 6–3. *A second skewer can add additional stability to kabobs.*

SPIT COOKING

Spit cooking is similar to stick cooking, but it usually involves larger portions of food. From Cornish game hens to whole chickens, from hams to whole pigs—all are adaptable to spit cooking.

Attach meat to the spit, centering and balancing it so that it turns evenly. If cooking poultry, secure the wings and legs firmly to the body so they do not stick out and burn. You may want to shield or cover protruding parts with foil to prevent overcooking.

Place the food on the spit above the coals and begin turning the handle. Medium-sized meat items like chickens should be cooked eight to ten inches from the coals. As with end-of-the-stick cooking, larger pieces should be cooked farther from the coals and smaller pieces should be cooked closer to them. Adjust the height of the spit if the meat is cooking too slowly or too quickly, and make sure the meat continues to turn slowly for even cooking.

Spits. A three-quarter-inch-diameter stick makes a good spit. A second, smaller stick can be lashed to this stick as a handle for easy turning. A metal pipe can also be used as a spit. Weld a handle on one end of the metal spit to help you turn it more easily. It's helpful to drill holes through the middle of the

Figure 6–4. *Bricks and dowels can be used to support and stabilize a spit.*

pipe so that meat can be secured to the pipe with wire. Determine the needed length of your spit by measuring the length of food you plan to cook and adding two to three feet.

Spit support. Use sturdy forked sticks to support the spit, or weld three U-shaped pieces of half pipe to the sides of two three-foot pieces of pipe. The U-shaped pieces serve as brackets, making it possible to adjust the height of the spit. You may also substitute stacked rocks or bricks to hold the spit. Select bricks that have holes in the center, stack them on opposite sides of the coals where the spit is to be supported, and suspend the spit across the middle.

Cooking temperature. Increase cooking temperature by removing one or more bricks to move food closer to your coals. To lower heat, add additional bricks underneath the spit to raise the food.

Marinating and basting. Before cooking meat on a spit, consider marinating it. Marinating tenderizes and adds flavor. Add a basting sauce for additional flavor when the meat has almost finished cooking.

ALUMINUM FOIL COOKING

I've been accused of owning an aluminum foil company because I use and recommend foil so much for outdoor cooking. One advantage of foil cooking is that it makes for easy food storage, preparation, cooking, and cleanup. Another advantage is that each young woman can assemble ingredients for her own meal, wrap it in foil, and cook it.

Aluminum foil dinners can be prepared, seasoned, and packed in advance of cooking. This cuts down on preparation time and gives everyone an activity. These dinners will hold their heat for up to fifteen minutes after being removed from the coals, and your young women will enjoy eating them directly out of the foil wrap.

Campers are experts at preparing and cooking the famous Hobo Dinner. My favorite is the foil-wrapped Banana Boat, which uses marshmallows and chocolate chips and cooks in a banana peel (see chapter 9 for recipes).

Aluminum foil is a versatile material for cooking and wrapping food. It is the modern version of cooking with leaves and clay. Introduced in 1947, aluminum foil has become an increasingly popular cooking material and a mainstay in every kitchen. It is 95 percent aluminum, with iron and silicon added to promote strength and puncture resistance. Heavier weights of foil are preferred for outdoor cooking because of their added strength.

Extra-heavy-duty aluminum foil can even be shaped into a homemade pan. Cut a piece of foil and place it inside a pan, molding it to the pan's shape. Then remove the foil from the pan, folding the excess foil down on the sides to give the foil pan extra durability. A homemade pan eliminates a dish to wash.

Figure 6–5. *Place food in the middle of one or two sheets of foil.*

Fold in half-inch intervals, starting at the ends and working toward the center.

Roll open ends toward the center to seal.

Drugstore Wrap

To prepare an aluminum foil dinner:

1. Wrap a piece of heavy-duty or extra-heavy-duty foil twice around the item to be cooked and then cut the foil.

2. Spread out the foil and arrange your food in its center.

3. Bring opposite sides of the foil together and fold down in small half-inch folds until package can no longer be folded.

4. Flatten the two sides of the package, then roll the open edges toward the center in small folds. The edges of the package must be tightly sealed to hold in heat and juices.

5. If the package needs to be wrapped again for strength, place the folded top of the package upside down in the center of another piece of foil and repeat.

Dutch Oven Cooking

The Dutch oven is the most versatile utensil for outdoor cooking. It uses either dry or moist heat in a variety of cooking techniques, including baking, stewing, braising, and frying, and can be used for main courses, side dishes, breads, and—best of all—desserts.

As one of the World Dutch Oven Cooking Contest judges for several years, I have tasted succulent shrimp, standing rib roasts, mouth-watering breads, and even perfect pies baked inside Dutch ovens. There's virtually no limit to Dutch oven uses for the creative outdoor cook.

Dutch ovens, one of the oldest cooking implements, are cast-iron pots ranging from five to sixteen inches in diameter. They hold heat well for long periods of time. Dutch ovens have been a staple of American cooking since the early history of the United States. They continue to be used today as an easy way to cook delicious meals.

Modern Dutch ovens began as black ironware, which was used throughout Europe for many years. England was a primary exporter of cast-iron pots, skillets, and kettles through its worldwide fleet. In early America, Dutch traders traveled door-to-door selling household goods, including baking ovens—hence the name, Dutch oven.

Family journals from early America tell of many people who relied on their cast-iron kettles and Dutch ovens for everyday cooking. Paul Revere is often credited with developing the flat-topped, three-legged Dutch oven.

Camp-Style Dutch Oven

The camp-style Dutch oven has three legs and a flanged lid. It is designed so that hot coals can be placed underneath and on top. A heavy metal handle is attached at two sides and curves over the top of the pot, making it easy to hang or carry the oven. A Dutch oven can be suspended over coals, placed on the ground over coals, buried underground in coals, or stacked on other Dutch ovens.

Purchase Dutch ovens from hardware stores, outdoor recreational stores, and other general retailers, or order them from mail-order vendors or from websites.

Kitchen-Style Dutch Oven

The kitchen-style Dutch oven has a flat bottom with no legs and a dome-shaped lid with no flange. It is designed to be used in a home oven, on a range, or on a camp stove. You can adapt it for outdoor use by hanging it from a tripod over coals or by elevating it above coals with rocks or bricks. To adapt the oven's lid to hold coals, turn it upside down. Or create a foil ring slightly smaller in circumference than the lid. Mold the foil ring onto the lid and arrange the coals inside the ring.

Choosing a Dutch Oven

If you plan to purchase a Dutch oven for camp, select it in accordance with how often you'll use it. The more you plan to use it (and you'll want to use it often after you've tasted some delicious Dutch oven dishes), the more you'll want to invest in a high-quality oven. With Dutch ovens, low price can mean low quality. Choose well-known, name-brand ovens.

Avoid ovens with riveted tabs. Make sure the bail handle is made of heavy gauge wire that is securely attached on each side of the oven. Choose ovens with lid handles that are attached to the lid on two sides of the lid. Avoid lids with skillet-type handles, which are more of a nuisance than a help.

If you plan on doing most of your camp cooking outside, purchase an oven with legs—ovens with three legs are easier to cook with than ovens with four legs. If you plan on cooking a variety of dishes simultaneously, buy several ovens with legs for easy stacking.

Dutch ovens are made of either cast iron or aluminum. Aluminum ovens heat up faster, weigh less, don't rust, and offer easier cleanup, but they don't retain their heat as long as cast iron ovens and require more coals to reach and maintain constant temperatures. In addition, aluminum ovens have a much lower melting point than cast iron ovens.

Sizes of Dutch Ovens

Dutch ovens come in a variety of sizes. Twelve-inch ovens are the best all-around size. They can accommodate most recipes and feed approximately fifteen people. Use smaller ovens for desserts, soups, vegetables, and main dishes for small groups; use larger, deeper ovens for roasts, turkeys, stews, and main dishes for large groups. Whatever size you choose, it's always a good idea to experiment with several ovens borrowed from family and friends before making your purchase.

People often ask me what size of Dutch oven they should buy. For a family of four, a ten- or twelve-inch oven is best. For a larger family, a twelve- or fourteen-inch oven is best. But for camp, I recommend eight-inch ovens. My experience with camping programs has taught me that if you have a ten-inch oven or larger, most of the time the leaders cook. I saw this happen over and over again at the Brighton Girls Camp, so I encouraged camp leaders to buy eight-inch ovens and develop recipes for them. We divided the young women into groups of two to four and had each group cook in one oven. Eventually the young women, rather than their leaders, did the cooking.

Remember, the camp experience is to help young women learn to do things for themselves and their families outdoors. Create activities, including cooking, that help young women develop self-reliance.

Seasoning and Reseasoning a Dutch Oven

Because cast iron is a porous metal, you must "season" it before using it. Wash the pot and lid with mild, soapy water and a stiff brush to dissolve the manufacturer's protective wax residue. (This is the only time you will use soap on your Dutch oven.) Wipe both the oven and lid dry.

Using a clean cloth or paper towel, grease the inside and outside or your oven and lid with one or two tablespoons of vegetable oil or shortening. Repeat the procedure, adding more oil as necessary. Be sure to wipe up any extra oil so that no pools of oil remain. A nonstick cooking surface will build up as you continue to give your Dutch oven an oil treatment after every use.

Next, preheat a conventional oven to 350 degrees. Place the Dutch oven upside down on a rack with a cookie sheet or piece of aluminum foil underneath it to prevent oil from dripping onto the heating elements. Place the lid atop the legs of the upside down pot.

Turn the oven off after an hour, but leave the Dutch oven inside until it cools completely. Never use water to speed the cooling process because it can cause the oven to pit or warp. After cooling, the oven is ready for cooking.

Cleaning and Storage

Keeping your Dutch oven clean is essential to enjoying your outdoor cooking experience. Use a rubber spatula, wooden spoon, or plastic scrubby (steel wool will remove your seasoning) to scrape out any food that remains in the oven. If food has hardened and baked onto the surface, add water and bring it to a boil until the food loosens and can be wiped off. Wiping with a mixture of salt or kosher salt and oil can help clean your oven without scratching it. After wiping the oven clean, dry it and apply a thin coat of oil to the entire surface with a paper towel.

To improve the flavor of future meals and to prolong the life of your oven, store it properly. Since moisture is your oven's greatest enemy, store the oven so that no moisture can remain inside. Loosely wad a handful of paper towels and place them inside the pot so they can absorb any remaining moisture. Also, roll some aluminum foil into a "snake" and arrange it as a collar on the rim of the pot, creating a space between the pot and the lid to allow moisture to evaporate.

If your Dutch oven is stored for long intervals, the oil may take on a gummy texture. If this occurs, heat the oven upside down on a cookie sheet at 350 degrees in your oven or over glowing briquettes until the residue melts. Then wipe it clean with a paper towel. If you buy a Dutch oven at a yard or garage sale that is so dirty or gummy that it cannot be cleaned by hand, place it in your self-cleaning conventional oven and run the self-cleaning cycle. You'll need to reseason your Dutch oven when you clean it this way, but all the dirt and oil will burn off.

With proper care, a Dutch oven will give you years of scrumptious meals and will always be ready for your next outdoor adventure.

Accessories

A wide array of accessories is helpful, and in some cases essential, to Dutch oven cooking. You will develop a list of your favorite accessories as you refine and personalize your cooking techniques. Meanwhile, consider the following:

Lid lifter. A lid lifter allows you to remove the lid without burning your hands. You can also use a pair of pliers or the claw end of a hammer.

Lid holder or rack. A rack keeps the lid clean while you're checking food or cooking without the lid.

Leather gloves, hot pads, oven mitts, cooking shirt (see chapter 3). These items allow you to work more freely around a Dutch oven without burning your hands.

Tongs. Tongs help you arrange hot briquettes.

Whisk broom. A whiskbroom is good for keeping briquette ashes off your Dutch oven lids.

Cutting board. A cutting board offers a clean surface to prepare food.

Shovel. A shovel can be used to clear a cooking area, move coals to and from an oven lid, and throw dirt on coals.

Dutch oven cooking table. This metal, fireproof table retains heat and provides a flat surface, making cooking easier and saving you from endless squatting, bending, and lifting.

Nylon storage bags. These lightweight storage bags keep your ovens and accessories clean.

Temperature Control

Virtually any method of cooking at home—baking, braising, boiling, frying, stewing, and roasting—can be duplicated by a Dutch oven. Many baking recipes require a temperature of 325–350 degrees, which is easily achieved in a Dutch oven. Simply add the number 3 to the diameter of your oven to determine the number of charcoal briquettes needed on top and subtract the number 3 from your oven's diameter to determine the number of briquettes needed underneath. The following chart shows the correct number of hot briquettes to use to generate 350 degrees.

NUMBER OF BRIQUETTES NEEDED TO GENERATE 350 DEGREES		
Size of Oven	Top	Bottom
8-inch	11	5
10-inch	13	7
12-inch	15	9
14-inch	17	11
16-inch	19	13

Following this formula, fifteen briquettes would go on top of a twelve-inch Dutch oven and nine briquettes would go underneath it to cook at 350 degrees. Heat rises, so you do not need as many coals on the bottom of the oven. To achieve higher temperatures, use additional coals on the lid and underneath. Arrange briquettes so they are evenly spaced. To avoid hot spots, every fifteen minutes you should rotate your Dutch oven about a third of a turn one way while rotating the lid about a third of a turn the other way. When baking cakes, breads, or rolls, remove the bottom coals about two-thirds of the way into the baking time. You may find that some cakes, breads, and rolls require fewer coals underneath your oven than suggested by the formula above. Replace briquettes with new coals before they burn out.

Baking in a Dutch Oven

Most people would never dream of baking outdoors, but you can bake flavorful treats in a Dutch oven. Cake, pie, and biscuits cooked in your kitchen take about the same time in a Dutch oven. Baking can be done directly in the bottom of

Figure 6–6. *Temperature control is determined by the number of charcoal briquettes placed underneath and on top of your Dutch ovens.*

a Dutch oven or by elevating a pan in an oven using rocks, canning jar rings, a trivet, a round cookie-cooling rack, or small wads of foil. When a pan is elevated in a Dutch oven, hot air can circulate around it just as it does in your oven at home.

To practice Dutch oven pie baking before going to camp, prepare a pie for baking. Then, using a twelve-inch Dutch oven, place eleven hot coals underneath the oven and seventeen on

Figure 6–7. *Use rocks to elevate baking pans for pies, cakes, or bread.*

Figure 6–8. *Pies bake perfectly inside a Dutch oven.*

the lid to generate 375 degrees. Place the prepared pie in the oven and bake thirty to forty minutes.

Roasting in a Dutch Oven

Most roasting recipes require a temperature of 375 degrees or higher. Preheat your Dutch oven for ten minutes before filling it. Remember to use eleven hot coals underneath the oven and seventeen on the lid to generate 375 degrees.

Frying in a Dutch Oven

To sauté food in a Dutch oven, place charcoal briquettes under the oven in a checkerboard pattern, using the same number of briquettes as the diameter of the Dutch oven. To fry foods in deep oil, add enough briquettes underneath the oven so that the oil becomes hot enough to fry.

Simmering in a Dutch Oven

To simmer foods, start with a 325-degree oven and let the coals cool as your food cooks. Do not replace the briquettes as they die down. Hot coals are enough to simmer foods for an hour to an hour and a half, especially when you tap the ashes off of the coals, which allows them to use more oxygen.

Stacking Dutch Ovens

When you're cooking several different dishes at the same time, stack the pots to save space and briquettes. Stacking works best if you put the food to be baked at the bottom of the stack and then add Dutch ovens containing food that requires shorter cooking times. Always start with the largest Dutch oven on the bottom and decrease oven size as you stack.

Figure 6–9. *Stack Dutch ovens for efficient and convenient cooking.*

GRILLING

The most popular form of outdoor cooking is grilling, or bar-becuing, especially at camp. Grilled meat, fish, and poultry may be familiar to your young women, but they've probably never enjoyed grilled fruit, vegetables, and desserts. For example, warm, juicy grilled pineapple chunks are a treat for everyone.

Grill cooking is versatile, convenient, fun, and easy— especially cleanup. The key to successful grilling is effectively regulating the heat. Cooking times vary depending on the temperature of the coals and the size, shape, cut, and type of food you're grilling.

Hibachis and kettle grills are equipped with air vents at the bottom to regulate oxygen. Opening the vents adds oxygen flow to the coals, increasing the heat; closing the vents shuts off oxygen flow, lowering the heat. If you're cooking on a grill with a lid, leaving the lid down allows heat to circulate and evenly cook the food without flare-ups. Lifting the lid increases cooking time. To help determine when your food is done, use a thermometer to measure the internal temperature.

Turning your food with tongs or turners rather than forks protects your food from being pierced, which can cause flavorful juices to escape. To make cleanup easier, coat the grill with oil or a nonstick vegetable spray before cooking. Trim excess fats from meat or select lean cuts to avoid flare-ups, which you can control with a squirt gun or spray bottle.

Before heading to camp, carefully review recipes. Better yet, try them out first at home during a Young Women activity. This will help you judge how hot your coals should be, how long your food should be grilled, and how your food should taste.

If you plan on using a basting sauce, preheat it to avoid slowing down your cooking. Because barbecue sauces often contain sugar that burns easily after caramelizing, it is best to baste

SAFE COOKING TEMPERATURES

Type of Meat	Temperature
Beef and Lamb	
Rare	140
Medium	160
Well-done	170
Chicken	175–180
Fish	120–145
Ground Meats	
Beef, lamb, pork	160
Chicken and turkey	165
Pork	
Chops, roast	150–165
Cured	140
Sausage	160
Turkey	
Bone-in	180
Boneless roast	170

during the last fifteen minutes so that the sauce won't burn or cause your food to burn.

Use long-handled tools, barbecue gloves, and a cooking shirt to protect your hands from the heat.

Mixed Grill

A combination of bacon, chicken, kielbasa or sausage, lamb chops, pork, steak, and tenderloin basted with barbecue sauce and served together is called a "mixed grill." It is frequently served with grilled vegetables. This is a nice menu choice because everyone gets to sample several different items.

READY-TO-EAT AND PREPARED FOODS

Grilled foods are fast, convenient, and satisfying. There's nothing better than a tender cut of meat grilled to perfection. When camping, however, consider taking advantage of time-saving shortcuts to grilling. Meat fully cooked ahead of time, for example, can be heated and ready to eat just a few minutes after you put it on the grill. Many meat products come packaged within their own sauce, which makes them even more convenient. Supermarkets feature a great variety of barbecued ribs (beef and pork), chicken breasts, whole chickens, pork tenderloins, and so forth ready for grill heating.

COOKING FISH

Fish cooks at a lower temperature than meat or poultry. A good rule for cooking fish is to measure the thickest part with a ruler and cook eight to ten minutes per inch of thickness. Fish can be baked, broiled, fried, grilled, and steamed. To test fish for doneness, flake it with a fork at its thickest point. It should be opaque, and the juices should be milky white. Overcooked fish is dry and falls apart easily. Another test is to insert a cooking thermometer at the thickest point. It should register 145 degrees when fish is fully cooked.

COOKING PORK

Pork is leaner and higher in protein than it was ten years ago and rarely tainted anymore with trichinosis. Nevertheless, don't taste uncooked pork, and wash anything that comes in contact with raw pork and other raw meats. An internal temperature of 137 degrees will kill trichinae, but an internal temperature of 150–165 degrees will add an increased safety margin. Your meat will be overcooked if you follow the 170–185 degrees recommended in many cookbooks.

NOVELTY COOKING

During countless television appearances over the years, I have found that my innovative novelty cooking ideas generated the most enthusiastic response of all my "roughing it" suggestions. Johnny Carson helped me cook bacon and eggs in a paper sack. Tom Brokaw prepared ice cream in a tin can. Jane Pauley boiled water in a paper cup. Martin Short, on the premiere episode of his television show, carried around a whole chicken as it cooked in his backpack. Share the inventive ideas that follow with your young women, and you'll generate as many memorable experiences as I have.

In outdoor cooking, it's fun to explore both a variety of cooking methods and a variety of utensils, including items that weren't originally designed as utensils. The possibilities for novelty cooking are limited only by your imagination. Try some of the following ideas, and create your own ideas for novelty cooking.

Cooking Food Inside Food

A unique way to both cook and flavor foods is to cook one food inside another. The outer food shields the inner food against extreme heat and gives additional flavor.

Cooking inside an orange. Select an orange with a thick peel because it is easier to remove the fruit inside. Cut the orange in half. Ease your fingers between the flesh and the peel of the orange. Slide your fingers back and forth to detach the flesh from the peel, leaving an orange "cup." You can also use a spoon to separate the fruit from the peel. Eat the pulp or use it in another recipe.

Eggs, muffins, or cupcakes all cook nicely inside the peel of an orange. For cupcakes and muffins, fill an orange cup two-thirds full with batter. Place the filled orange cup on a square of

Figure 6–10. *Poor cake into an orange peel, wrap, and cook.*

Figure 6–11. *A muffin in one orange peel and an egg in another make a fun breakfast.*

aluminum foil. Pull the foil over the cup and twist it at the top to leave room for the batter to rise inside the cup as it cooks. Place it on hot coals for about ten minutes.

Just for fun, cook an egg in one half of the orange and muffin batter in the other half for a quick breakfast. Gingerbread and chocolate cake are also especially delicious this way.

Cooking inside an onion. See one of my signature recipes in chapter 9 for cooking meatloaf in an onion. This is a wonderful recipe for large groups because each young woman makes her own.

Boiling Water in a Paper Cup

It's possible to boil water in an unwaxed paper cup without the cup igniting. Pour water or milk into the cup. Cut a small square of aluminum foil and place it under the cup. Set the foil and cup in or on hot coals. The foil protects the small lip on the cup's bottom from burning. If flames rise against the top of the cup where liquid does not reach, the cup can burn.

Figure 6–12. *You really can boil water in a paper cup.*

97

Another way to boil water in a paper cup is to place the cup on a buddy burner (see chapter 5). Stir in ingredients to create your favorite hot beverage, such as hot chocolate. Or throw in an egg and enjoy a soft- or hard-cooked egg for breakfast. It's also possible to heat a carton of milk if the carton is unwaxed. Open the milk carton top before heating.

Breakfast Cooked in a Paper Bag

To cook bacon and eggs for breakfast, cut a strip of bacon in half. Spread it in the bottom of a new lunch-sized paper sack. Break one or two eggs and drop them on top of the bacon inside the sack. To make scrambled eggs, open and fold down the top of the bag. Then crack the shells of the eggs, hold them high over the bag, and release. When they'll hit the bottom of the bag, they'll be scrambled.

Beginning at the bag's top, roll it down in one-inch folds until you reach its middle. Poke a stick through the rolled folds at the top of the sack and hold it over a bed of coals, or set it on a tin-can stove or on a piece of foil above a bed of hot coals. Grease will appear along the bottom of the bag as the food cooks. The bacon and eggs will cook in approximately ten minutes.

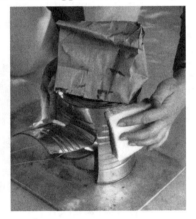

Figure 6–13. *Enjoy eggs and bacon cooked in a paper bag with "a side" of toast.*

Leaf Cooking

A quick and easy "pan" for cooking ground beef is a cabbage leaf. Shape a ground beef patty, set it on the leaf, and place the leaf onto hot coals. The edges of the leaf will turn brown, but the center will remain firm. With a spatula and a hot pad, turn the meat over on the leaf when it's halfway done.

Cardboard Box/Foil Oven

The efficiency of this oven will delight you. It will bake a cake as well as your oven at home. And the oven is fun to make as an activity before camp.

1. Cut the top off of a cardboard box that is approximately one foot square. (The box should be about one inch larger all the way around than the baking pan that will be used inside of it.) With the top cut off, lay the box on its side. The cut-off portion of the box will be the opening to the oven.

2. Line the entire inside of the box with foil.

3. Close all seams on the outside of the box with duct tape (heat-resistant tape) to keep heat from leaking out.

4. Punch two quarter-inch holes in the sides of the box near the bottom for ventilation. (If your coals begin to die while your food is baking, you may have to punch more holes.)

5. Punch two small holes quite close together at the back, high in one corner. Run a twist tie (from a plastic bag) through the holes and tie a thermometer to the inside of the box.

6. For the door of the oven, cut a piece of cardboard a quarter inch larger than the opening to the oven.

Figure 6–14. *The efficiency of a cardboard box/foil oven is amazing.*

Line the inside of the door with foil. On the outside of the door, tape a handle shaped from a piece of cardboard.

7. If you want a window in the oven door, cut a square hole in the door and cover it with transparent oven wrap secured by the duct tape.

8. Secure the door to the top of the opening with duct tape so the door swings upward, as if it were hinged.

9. For the oven rack, use a metal rack about 20 inches long and 6 inches wide. Fold both ends of the rack about 4½ inches from the ends at right angles so that your rack's flat surface will be 11 inches. Stand the rack inside the oven.

10. For insulation, pour pebbles or dirt into a pan that will fit into the bottom of the oven. Place fifteen to twenty hot briquettes on top of the pebbles. (Foil can be placed across the dirt or sand to elevate the briquettes, giving them more oxygen).

When you're ready to use the oven, preheat it to the desired temperature. When you place food on the rack, the oven's temperature will decrease temporarily but should rise again as the food cooks. Place a rock against the outside of the oven door to keep it closed. A small gap is okay, but large spaces will let heat escape. The briquettes

Figure 6–15. *Cook yummy cakes in a cardboard box oven.*

will hold their heat for about an hour. If you expect to use the oven for a longer period of time, add briquettes gradually while the first ones are still hot.

Cardboard Box Oven with a Window

Cut the top and bottom from a cardboard box about a foot square and fourteen inches deep. Cover the bottom edge of the cardboard box with aluminum foil so it will be protected from the heat of the coals. Dig a trench eight inches deep, eight inches wide, and about twenty inches long. Place charcoal briquettes in one end of the trench and light them, or place briquettes on a backpacker's rack as shown in Figure 6–17.

Figure 6–17. *Add a window to your cardboard box oven so you can watch food cook.*   Figure 6–18. *Bread bakes perfectly in a cardboard box oven with a window.*

Place a cooling rack in the middle of the box. Then poke a hole above and below each corner of the rack and wire it in place. Place the box over the charcoal briquettes in the open trench, which extends from under the box and admits air to the coals. The edge of the box, though it is reinforced with additional foil, should be kept away from direct heat as much as possible.

Place the item to be baked or roasted on the rack and cover the box with a roasting wrap (secured with either string or a rubber band) so you can see the food baking. Aluminum foil can be used, but it won't allow you to watch the food cooking. The oven can be lifted on and off the coals as needed. If desired, a portable oven thermometer can be hung on the upper inside of the box to monitor the oven temperature.

Pie-Tin Oven

Two pie tins can be used to make an oven that will bake biscuits, pies, cake, pizza, and other foods.

1. Oil one pie tin and place food in it.

2. Turn a second pie tin upside down over the first tin to make a lid.

3. Use three or four metal clips (such as Bulldog clips used to clamp paper together) an equal distance apart on the lip of the pans.

4. Situate three rocks or spikes in a bed of coals so that they elevate the pie-tin oven one inch above the coals.

5. Place coals on the lid. If more coals are needed than will fit over the lid, make a collar by folding a length of foil two or three times and hooking it together at the ends around the pie tin.

6. Charcoal briquettes get very hot, so place them in a checkerboard pattern, leaving plenty of space between them. Brush them off before opening the lid. Cooking time should be about the same as it would be in a home oven. You will need pliers or heatproof gloves to remove the clips.

Solar Cooking

Solar cooking offers numerous advantages. The sun becomes your fuel source and is available anywhere and anytime it shines. Once you've read this chapter, you'll be able to cook meals without electricity or a fire pit. It's amazing to see how many great recipes can be used with solar cookers.

Solar cooking offers many advantages:

- Most solar cookers have gentle cooking temperatures, so foods retain more of their flavor, moisture, and nutrients, and they rarely overcook or burn. Cooking gently for many hours makes meats especially tender. In clear weather, a solar stove will amaze even the most skeptical observer. But when the sun goes down, so does your heat source, and on a rainy day, the solar cooker is not much use.

- As you'll discover when you hold your hand close to the

focal point, there is no warming-up period with a solar stove—it is hot right away!

- Solar energy is free anywhere the sun shines, and solar energy takes nothing from the environment.
- Solar cooking is safe because the heat goes into the food, not the person cooking it.
- Solar cooking doesn't require matches.
- Solar cooking requires no cleanup, and there's no danger of setting anything on fire. You'll probably have so much fun cooking with sunshine that you'll want to use a solar stove during your next camp.

Types of Solar Cookers

There are several types of solar cookers, including heat-trap boxes, curved-reflector concentrators, and combinations of those two types.

CooKit. My favorite and the easiest to make and use is the CooKit. It has many of the advantages of boxes and concentrators without most of their disadvantages. The CooKit doesn't need to be adjusted during several hours of cooking, is stable in wind, needs no window or insulation materials, is affordable, is easy

Figure 6–19. *CooKit fold-able solar cooker.*

to make, and folds flat for easy carrying and storing. It does require special transparent plastic bags (oven roasting bags), which are reusable up to ten times.

Box-type. The box-type is the most widely used solar cookers in households. In India, hundreds of thousands of people use them.

Curved concentrators more closely duplicate fire cooking, reach extreme temperatures, and require more constant attention.

103

About 150,000 are reportedly in use in homes in western China.

Foldable Solar Cooker. A handy, tuck-under-your-arm-or-in-your-backpack cooker requires a longer cooking time than the curved solar cooker but can cook for four to six people. The foldable solar cooker can be left to cook for hours without your having to watch or stir the cooking food or adjust the cooker's position in relation to the sun. Moving the cooker every few hours, however, will speed up the cooking time. Think "solar crockpot." Foods cook gently in their own juices, and breads and cakes bake to perfection.

Figure 6–20. *Box-type solar cooker.*

Figure 6–21. *Curved solar cooker.*

To cook with a foldable solar cooker, you'll need an outdoor spot that is sunny for several hours and protected from wind, animals, and children.

Enclose the pot in a high-temperature transparent plastic bag (oven bag) to let in the sunlight and retain heat around the pot. Put a pot stand under the pot to help reduce heat loss from the bottom. This can be a cloth, wire rack, two small sticks, or three small stones.

Making a Foldable Solar Cooker

To make a foldable solar cooker, you will need:

- Cardboard (3x4 feet)
- Cutting knife
- Aluminum foil—enough to cover one side of the cardboard

- White craft glue-water mix: one part glue to one part water

Cut and fold cardboard as shown in Figure 6.22. Make the slots in the front panel narrow so the front corners of the walls fit snugly and hold up the front panel. To make clean straight folds in cardboard, make a crease along the line with a blunt edge, such as a table knife or spoon handle. Then fold against a firm, straight edge.[1] Spread the glue mixture on aluminum foil and smooth onto one side of the cardboard. Leave flat until dry.

Cooking with a Solar Cooker

- Solar cooking takes several hours, so plan ahead.
- Set up the reflector and anchor it with large stones or bricks if there is wind.
- Put food in a dark cooking pan or jar with a tight-fitting lid. Wide, shallow pots are best; food should be no deeper than a hand's width.

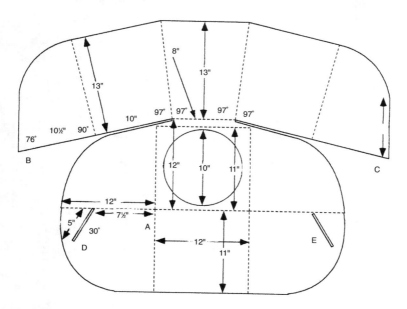

Figure 6–22. CooKit plans for a foldable solar cooker.

- Put the pot inside a large oven bag, and place it in the center of the reflector.
- Adjust the front flap to shine the most light onto the pot (lower when the sun is low, higher when the sun in high).
- Nearly any recipe requiring boiling, roasting, or baking gets excellent results in a solar cooker.
- Foods cut into small pieces cook faster than large pieces.

Solar cooking allows great flexibility. Solar-cooked food seldom overcooks. Foods cook fastest when the sun is highest (midday). Solar cookers will not work during the early morning, on cloudy days, or in the late afternoon.

Start your noon meal early in the morning and your evening meal about noon. The higher the sun, the shorter the cooking time. Thus, the optimal cooking time is midday. If your shadows are longer than you are, cooking time will be extended. For cooking large quantities, you can jumpstart the cooking by pre-heating food on another stove or dividing it up to cook in several solar cookers.

Here are some suggestions for cooking with a solar cooker:

Cereals, grains, barley, corn, millet, oats, rice, and wheat. Combine them with water and cook without stirring. If the texture

USUAL COOKING TIMES FOR FOUR POUNDS OF FOOD ON A SUNNY DAY		
Quick *1–2 hours*	Medium *3–4 hours*	Long *5–8 hours*
Eggs	Potatoes	Large roasts
Rice	Root vegetables	Soup and stew
Fruit	Some beans, lentils	Most dried beans
Vegetables	Most meats	
Fish	Bread	
Chicken		

is too soft or dry, adjust the amount of water the next time you prepare it.

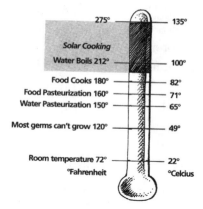

Figure 6–23. *Solar cooking temperatures.*

Vegetables and rice. Mix vegetables with rice and water. Add favorite seasonings to taste. If your vegetables are fresh, use a little less water and cook about three hours. For chicken and rice, put raw chicken pieces on top of the rice and cook at least two hours. Add about one-fourth less water than you would normally use for cooking rice.

Pastas. Cook as usual, but use less water. Put water into the cooker, and when water is near boiling, add pasta, stir, and cook about fifteen minutes.

Beans (dried). For faster cooking, soak beans in water overnight. Some beans cook in three to five hours; others, especially in large quantities, take all day. Don't add salt until beans are cooked. For the last one to two hours, add tomatoes and onions.

Fresh meats, vegetables, and fruits. Add little or no water. They cook in their own juices. The longer meat cooks, the more tender it becomes.

Pot roast. A super one-pot meal can be made by cooking the roast with potatoes, carrots, onions, turnips, celery, zucchini, mushrooms, and tomatoes or tomato sauce. Cut up the meat and cook for three to four hours. Add vegetables, herbs, and spices and cook an additional one to two hours or until tender.

Vegetable greens. Most greens cook in less than two hours. If they're cooked longer, they lose their green color but generally retain their flavor.

Corn on the cob. Place corn on the cob in a jar (add no water), screw on the lid loosely, and cook about half an hour. If you prefer, leave corn in the husks and cook in a black cloth.

Stewed tomatoes. Slice tomatoes into quarters and place in a pan. Sprinkle fine bread crumbs and cheddar cheese on top. Sprinkle with salt, pepper, and basil or other favorite herbs. Cover and bake about two hours.

Whole potatoes. Wash potatoes and oil the skins if you like them soft, then put them in a black pot with a lid or in a jar with a lid. Cooking time is usually three hours.

Fruit. Wash fruit and remove peels, pits, and cores. Then cut up the fruit and place it in a pan. Sprinkle with sugar and cinnamon. Bake 1½ hours. Optional meringue topping: Beat three egg whites until stiff, adding one teaspoon of vanilla and three-quarters cup of sugar while beating. Spread on top of cooked fruit. Return to solar box and bake uncovered one hour. Serve hot or cold.

Breads, cakes, pastries. Bake in a covered black pan in the middle of the day (between 10 A.M. and 2 P.M.). Cookies don't need a cover. Bake bottom crusts (pies, pizzas) alone and heat fillings separately, combining just before eating. Flat breads (tortillas, pancakes) and deep-fried foods or pastries with bottom crusts do not fare well with solar cooking.

Eggs. Cook in shells without water for one to two hours. With longer cooking, egg whites tend to "tan" but do not lose flavor.

Gravies. Mix drippings with flour or cornstarch. Add water or milk to mixture and stir until smooth. Return mixture to solar cooker, where it will quickly thicken.

Solar Cooker Food Safety

Meats, poultry, and fish must reach an internal temperature of 160 degrees Fahrenheit to kill disease-causing microorganisms such as salmonella and E-coli. Because foods cook in a solar oven at 180–195 degrees, they are safe to eat when fully cooked.

Soon after food is put into a solar cooker, temperatures will rise to above 120 degrees. The pot will be uncomfortably hot to touch, and germs stop growing.

If cooked food cools down to room temperature for several hours, it can spoil. When clouds come or after the sun sets, foods stay hot for only a short while in the CooKit but up to two hours in the solar box. Any cooked food that cools off and stays at room temperature for four hours or longer should be heated again to full cooking temperatures to destroy food-poisoning potential.

Other Uses for Solar Cookers

Heating water. Heating water takes a while, but it gets quite warm.

Drying foods. A foldable solar cooker can hasten the sun drying of small quantities of food. Put food on a wire rack or mesh screen in the reflector. The glare of the reflectors tends to keep insects away.

Disinfecting medical supplies. Dry heat destroys nearly all organisms, including many spores. Large solar cookers can easily reach 300 degrees, so in difficult field conditions, "baking" medical instruments, bandages, and other cloth materials in a dark container inside a plastic bag in a solar cooker can save lives.

REFLECTOR OVEN

Campers who roast or bake foods in a reflector oven are in for a real treat. This is one of the few methods of outdoor cooking in which the cook can watch the cooking process.

A reflector oven operates with a concentration of dry heat. This outdoor method closely duplicates the process of the oven in your home: dry heat is created and then reflected from the walls of your oven around the food. Similarly, heat from the open fire is reflected off foil, metal, or rock into the oven and from the sides of the reflector oven.

The best type of fire for a reflector oven is a tepee fire. If the wind is blowing, or if your fire is small, build a fire reflector on the side

Figure 6–24. *Reflector oven.*

of the fire opposite the reflector oven. This will help reflect the heat from the fire back into the oven. A fire or heat reflector can be built in any of the following ways:

- Build the fire close to a rock. The rock will reflect heat into the reflector oven.
- Stack up a wall of rocks to reflect the heat.
- If two reflector ovens are available, place them so they face each other across the fire. This will provide maximum reflection.
- Construct a heat reflector by placing two sticks securely in the ground side-by-side and stretching foil between them.

Types of Reflector Ovens

You may purchase a reflector oven or construct one at home or camp. Commercial ovens usually fold up and transport easily, and some home-constructed reflector ovens can be made to collapse. The type of reflector oven you decide to make will determine what supplies you need.

Cookie sheet reflector oven. To make this oven, you will need five straight-edged cookie sheets, three metal rings, a drill, and small bolts or wires. Three cookie sheets hinged together like a book make the top, bottom, and center shelf of the oven. The other two sheets make up the oven's sides. Bolt the sides of the top and bottom (which are at right angles to each other and at a 45-degree angle to the ground) to the sides of the oven. Bolt the sides of the horizontal center shelf to the sides of the oven.

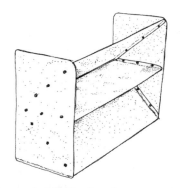

Figure 6–25. *Cookie sheet reflec-tor oven.*

Sheet metal reflector oven. To make this oven, you will need sheet metal, three metal rings, aluminum foil, green sticks, a drill, and stiff, heavy wire.

Cut three rectangles of sheet metal of equal size and attach them together along one long side with metal rings. Open the three metal sheets so the top and bottom sheets are at right angles to each other and the center sheet is horizontal. Holding each sheet in this position, lash each (with wire inserted through holes drilled in the corners of the sheets) to metal

Figure 6–26. *Sheet metal reflector oven.*

stakes or green sticks set in the ground on either side of the reflector oven. Cover the open sides of the oven with foil for additional reflected heat.

Keep the reflector ovens clean and shiny to create the most effective heat reflection. If the metal won't clean well, cover the oven with the shiny side of the aluminum foil outward so that it will reflect better.

Any foods that can be baked in thirty minutes or less in an oven can be baked outdoors in a reflector oven. Cookies, brownies, biscuits, pizza, and cake are favorites.

Cooking with a Reflector Oven

Place the food on a piece of foil or a pan that will fit on the shelf of the reflector oven, and then place the oven near the fire. Knowing just where to place the reflector oven so it will heat to the right temperature is the real key to cooking effectively. An oven thermometer inside the oven works well. Do not place it on top of the oven because it will catch the rising hot air and register a higher temperature than the shelf temperature.

After the food has been cooking for five minutes, check it to make sure that it is cooking properly by lifting the oven away from the fire area. Sometimes the food cooks faster at the front of the oven than it does at the back. If this happens, check to make sure that the oven is not too hot. Turn the food occasionally so it will cook evenly. If the top of the food is browning faster than the bottom, the fire is too large. Similarly, the fire is too small if foods are browner on the bottom than on the top.

Reflector ovens do best with foods that cook in less than twenty minutes.

PIT COOKING

Although it takes time and effort to dig a pit and prepare coals and ingredients for pit cooking, the work is done once the food has been placed in the pit. Food wrapped in foil or leaves or placed in a Dutch oven cooks well in a pit. This is one of the few outdoor methods good for cooking large items such as whole chickens, hams, turkeys, or roasts. By layering foods in the pit— meats, then potatoes, then vegetables, then desserts—you can cook a whole meal underground.

With pit cooking, heat is retained in the rocks and coals buried in the ground just as heat is retained in an oven at home. The main difference is the variation of heat. The pit starts very hot and gradually cools, while an oven retains constant heat. Foods can be cooked to perfection in a pit even with this variance in heat.

Preparing an Underground Pit

1. Dig a hole two to three times larger than the Dutch oven or the total size of the foil packages that will go into the pit. The rocks and packages of food that go into the pit should be surrounded by two to three inches of coals.

2. Line the pit with flat rocks. Don't use rocks that retain moisture, such as those from streambeds or those made of limestone or sandstone. They may explode.

3. Build a crisscross fire that will produce many coals. Burn logs two to four inches in diameter. Unless you want an extremely hot pit for cooking a turkey or a pig, logs larger than four inches in diameter will take too long to burn down.

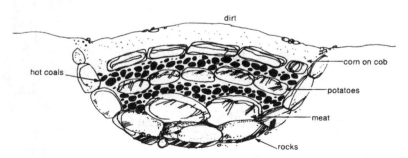

Figure 6–27. *Underground pit cooking.*

Because you will need lots of coals, add logs to the fire as it burns. It takes about an hour to heat rocks and fill the pit with coals and ashes. When the pit is almost filled with coals, it is ready for food to be placed in it.

Foods to Pit Cook

Pit cooking is an excellent method for cooking complete meals, including roast, ham, poultry, potatoes, corn on the cob, vegetables, and desserts. Here are some pit-cooking tips.

- Prepare foods for the pit while the fire is burning down by wrapping them in two layers of heavy-duty foil. The drugstore wrap technique (page 83) should be used for sealing food.

- Remove the hot coals from the center of the pit with a shovel and place them to the side. Don't spread the coals out any more than necessary because you will waste some of the heat.

- Place each wrapped item in the pit according to the length of time it requires for cooking. Each item needs to be completely covered with coals. Two packages that touch each other won't cook well. Items requiring a longer cooking time should be placed near the bottom of the pit, whereas those requiring a shorter cooking time will cook more slowly near the surface of the pit. A thin layer of dirt can be shoveled over the coals between two items of food to cut down the heat. It will take practice to cook well this way because temperatures and times vary depending on the type of wood and the amount of coals used.

- Place a section of newspaper over the coals before covering them with dirt. When you dig up the pit later, the newspaper will indicate that you are getting closer to the food.

- To make the coals steam, put wet burlap over the pit before covering the coals with dirt.
- Cover coals in the pit with four to six inches of dirt. A fire built over the pit will increase the temperature inside the pit.
- Allow meat about the size of a chicken to cook from 3 to 3½ hours. Subtract or add time to this amount for smaller or larger items. Cut a large roast into smaller pieces to reduce cooking time.
- When the allotted time is up, carefully remove the food from the pit with a shovel. Be careful not to pierce or cut into the food packages. Use gloves to remove the packages. For easy removal of large foil packages, wrap them with wire long enough to protrude from the top of the pit. This will allow you to locate the packages without breaking the foil with a shovel.

---

[1] To buy a foldable solar cooker or for more information on solar cookers and solar cooking, contact Solar Cookers International, 1919 21st Street, Suite 101, Sacramento, CA 95814 USA, or visit www.solarcooking.org/sci_orderform. Solar Cooker International, a mostly volunteer, educational, nonprofit organization, sells solar cookers, cookbooks, and educational materials related to solar cooking. Proceeds and contributions help Solar Cooker International provide solar cookers and training for refugees in East Africa and other sunny, fuel-scarce regions of the world.

CHAPTER 7

ACTIVITIES

The most successful activities at any camp are geared around the camp's environment. Mountain canyons, arid deserts, lakeside plains, or sandy beaches offer a multitude of recreation possibilities. Clever leaders will plan activities as an extension of the surroundings, carefully considering the climate, terrain, and other elements of the landscape.

Sharing a love of the outdoors can teach young women to respect the environment and enable them to return regularly to recapture the spirit of life outdoors. Many seasoned campers began to love nature during their first girls camp experience. A few well-planned activities can help young women discover the miracles found only in nature and can turn small moments into a lifetime of treasured memories.

CAMP JOURNALS

Some young women have reportedly claimed that the best part of camp is when it's over. From a positive perspective, this can be true if each young woman carries the memories of a meaningful activity, the fun of friendships made or enhanced, and the self-assurance from learning new skills. Girls camp can offer amazing new insights and memories for young women to recall the rest of their lives. One of the best ways to preserve the flavor, feeling, perspectives, and life-changing experiences of camp is to keep a journal.

Written journals and suggestion journals record events and activities but can also offer glimpses of special feelings, thoughts, and impressions. Photo journals provide a lasting record of the scenery, activities, and friendships formed at camp. Many artistic campers have used picture journals. Encourage campers to select their desired method in advance and to create a personal record of their camp experience.

Have the young women bring journals to camp, or provide them with paper to start one. Give them standard-size paper, such as 5-by-7 or 8½-by-11-inch sheets, so they can put the pages in a binder.

Schedule time each day for the young women to write in their journals. For example, set aside time after the flag ceremony in the morning, during the dinner hour in the evening, or just before bedtime.

Suggestion Journals

A written journal is the most common type of journal, but sometimes the young women have a hard time starting one because they don't know what to write about. A suggestion journal can help because it gives them things about which to write. Consider making a handout with the following suggestions:

- Dates of camp:
- Location:
- Description of camp:
- Tent mates:
- Camp leaders:
- What I discovered today in nature:
- What I discovered today about myself:
- What I discovered about my leaders:
- What I discovered about my tent mates:

- A fun thing that happened on the way to camp:
- A funny thing that happened at camp today was:
- How I helped someone today:
- I participated in these special activities:
- A new adventure I would like to have tomorrow is:
- A skill I learned today that I would like to share with my family is:

Picture Journals

Many young women can draw better than they can write. A picture journal gives them a chance to combine drawings and writing. A picture journal is a collection of drawings and sentences. For example, a picture journal might contain the following sentences with accompanying drawings:

- "Today we drove to camp in an old bus" (drawing of bus).
- "My leader is Sister Smith" (drawing of leader).
- "This evening we had a great campfire program" (drawing of campfire).
- We are camping in large tents (drawing of tent).
- This afternoon we saw a beautiful deer (drawing of deer).
- Our camp is surrounded by tall pine trees (drawing of trees).

Photo Journals

Another good idea is to have each young woman bring a disposable camera. Each time a camper takes a picture, she writes in her journal a description of the picture and what was happening, leaving space on a journal page to mount the picture when it is developed.

A great activity that goes with photo journals is having someone give instructions on how to take good pictures. A young woman in my area participated in an activity like this and later won a purple ribbon after entering one of her pictures in the state fair.

HIKING

There are several different types of hikes young women may enjoy at camp: day hikes, night hikes, sunrise hikes, nature hikes, theme hikes, and backpacking hikes. Good physical health, drinking water, and comfortable shoes or boots are the only real requirements for a successful hike. But a little creativity and a slightly different approach to hiking can ensure lasting memories from a routine part of outdoor recreation.

Day Hikes

A typical day hike can be enhanced with special snacks, plenty of water, compasses, and means of marking the trail. A long day hike offers a perfect opportunity to observe and identify the flora and fauna of your particular region and climate.

Day hikes are fun because the young women can see where they're going. With the wonders of nature surrounding them, they become part of nature. Day hikes offer opportunities to teach young women to respect and honor God's beautiful creations as leaders encourage them to take only pictures and leave only tracks.

Night Hikes

If you plan a night hike, be sure every young woman has a flashlight. Night hikes provide a perfect opportunity to identify stars and constellations.

On a night hike it is fun to have the young women all sit together and then turn off their flashlights. A night hike is a good time to talk about senses other than sight and to listen for animals and the sounds of wind and rustling leaves. Discuss the importance of light.

Sunrise Hikes

If you're camping in a mountainous area, it's fun to get the young women up before sunrise and hike to the top of a mountain to celebrate the sunrise. Don't forget to bring along some food.

Nature Hikes

Nature hikes require a little preparation and an understanding of the environment, but they offer a real opportunity to learn about the nearly limitless beauties of nature along the trail. Teach each camper to see nature's small surprises. Take time to observe and learn the names of flowers, trees, plants, and birds. Bring along binoculars and a botanical book, and teach the young women about the creatures and plants that surround them. Point out animal tracks and be prepared to share your outdoor knowledge. Better yet, invite someone knowledgeable about nature to join your young women on a nature hike and teach them about the plants and animals they encounter.

Plant identification hikes are always fun, especially if the leader can provide some background information and stories about the plants. For example, the broad, soft leaves of some wild berry bushes make great emergency outdoor toilet paper. Stinging nettle, on the other hand, makes nutritious cooked greens when the leaves are cooked to soften and disarm their stingers. Be careful not to mix up the two.

During a nature hike, give each young woman a yard or two of string. Then ask them to encircle an area on the ground with the string. They'll be amazed at how much life they encounter in such a small area and will enjoy counting the plants, insects, and other life forms they find within their circle.

Theme Hikes

Theme hikes require creativity but can generate incredible memories. Hiking blindfolded with a guide or hiking with a partner or in a small group teaches all sorts of team-building lessons along the trail. Backpacks are ideal for carrying games,

Black bear

front foot
3½ inches wide

Mountain lion
(Cougar)

front foot
3¾ inches wide

Moose

front foot
5¼ inches
long

3¼ inches long

Deer

Coyote

front foot
2 inches wide

Raccoon

hind foot
3⅛ inches long

121

projects, and meals to add to the fun and festive nature of any theme hike.

One example of a theme hike is the blind hike. Have the young women pair off, with one of them blindfolded. The one who is not blindfolded holds the arm of her partner and takes her for a walk. The goal is to stop several times and have the blindfolded young woman touch and smell items from nature, such as wood, leaves, and pine needles. It's also fun to see if she can identify the items.

Backpacking Hikes

Perhaps the greatest joy of backpacking springs from the sense of privacy and oneness with nature. Backpackers are dependent on the elements and must assume responsibility for themselves and for their environment. Because of this, the question for backpackers is, "How little can I take along and still have everything I need?"

Packs

Backpacking packs are larger than daypacks and contain more features. They come with either external or internal frames.

For overnight trips on established trails, an external frame pack with a heavy-duty frame and sturdy full-sized bag is a good choice. Such packs provide a broad base of support, allowing more variance in weight distribution and making it possible for hikers to carry heavy loads in an upright position, with most of the weight being supported by the hips. They are cooler because they don't press against the body.

Your external frame pack should have a frame made of lightweight aluminum, a hip belt, generously padded shoulder straps, a sternum strap, and load-lifter straps.

Packs usually have six to eight outside compartments for separating gear and making it easy to access. A good pack allows adjustment of both frame and bag to provide the correct fit. The bag should be attached to the frame with clevis pins and locking wire, not with flimsy cord loops sewn to the bag.

Internal frame packs are more expensive and can be heavier than external frame packs. They sit directly against the back, which makes them better for rough terrain but warmer during hot weather.

It's a good idea for young women and their leaders to keep their packs light (thirty to forty pounds for an adult woman). The pack weight a young woman can carry depends on her physical condition and experience, the terrain to be covered, the length of the trip, and the weather.

When packing, three important considerations to keep in mind are organizing the equipment, providing easy access to important articles, and distributing the load for maximum comfort and efficiency.

Nylon ditty bags and plastic sacks are helpful for organizing and protecting gear. They also help keep items compact and easy to reach. Pack rain gear and tents so they are easily accessed. Frequently used items, such as water bottles and snacks, should be placed in outside pockets or near pack openings. Large or bulky items, such as tent poles, sleeping bags, or sleeping pads, can be lashed to the pack or held on with compression straps.

The most important consideration in packing is centering the load over your vertical walking axis, or center of gravity. Avoid weighing down the lower portion of your pack. Too much weight too low will cause an unnatural pull on your back and strain both your back and leg muscles. When your load is correctly centered, it will normally ride fairly high on your back.

In loading your pack for trail hiking, place heavy items higher and closer to your back, lighter items lower and farther away from your back, and your sleeping bag at the bottom. For hiking off trails, pack lighter items higher and farther from your back, heavier items lower and closer to your back, and the sleeping bag on top.

Practice hoisting your pack without help from another person. Using your knee or bent leg as support will help. When the pack is on, the weight should fall naturally onto your hips. Be sure the shoulder straps are tight enough to keep the pack in line and the weight close to your back.

Equipment

Simplicity, lightness, and versatility are the watchwords of backpacking equipment.

- A two–three quart pot is sufficient for a party of two or three people. Nesting pans and plates saves space and weight.
- A stainless steel cup with a heat-resistant handle can be used for drinking, holding soup or stew, measuring, and cooking small amounts of food.
- A polycarbonate water bottle is light and unbreakable. Wide-mouth bottles are easiest to clean and can be used for mixing foods.
- Utensils should include a nesting steel knife-fork-spoon set, a can opener, and a good pocketknife.
- Backpacking tents weigh only a few pounds, but they're not cheap. For a backpacking trip in good weather, a simple shelter constructed of a tarp, poncho, or ground cloth tied between two trees may be sufficient.
- A lightweight sleeping bag is essential. Your bag must have maximum warmth but minimum bulk and weight. Sleeping bags are rated for warmth, although ratings are general and metabolisms vary.
- A sleeping pad provides insulation from cold ground. Self-inflating insulated pads are best for backpacking.

Food

Being creative in planning and cooking lightweight meals out-of-doors can be wonderfully rewarding—or frustrating and expensive if you don't have the know-how. For excellent eating on the trail, I recommend a combination of supermarket foods, fresh foods that travel well, and home-dried foods.

Plan simple breakfasts with hot cereal or hot chocolate for cold mornings, lunches that can be eaten along the trail, and dinners that can be prepared in one dish. In creating daily menus, plan for a variety of flavors (include sweet, spicy, bland, and so forth) and textures (crunchy, soft, chewy). Eating the same foods repeatedly can get old fast.

Here are some tips for preparing foods on the trail:

1. Reconstitute dehydrated vegetables during your lunch break by adding water to them in a heavy-duty plastic bag. Squeeze out the air and put the bag into another bag for added protection. The vegetables will be reconstituted by the time you're ready to prepare dinner.

2. Keep a folded plastic bag in your pocket. When you find a source of clean water, fill the bag and add a water-purification tablet. You can also purchase portable water-purification devices and specialized water carrying bags.

3. Mix foods such as cake mixes, pancake mixes, and meatloaf in heavy, reclosable plastic bags. Place the items in a bag, set the bag on a flat surface, squeeze out the excess air, and zip the bag shut. Holding the bag in one hand, squeeze the food with the other hand until it is properly mixed.

4. Make gelatin desserts on the trail by dissolving the gelatin in a reclosable plastic bag, removing as much air as possible. Then set the bag in a cool place, such as a stream, until it is set.

5. Use instant food from the grocery store rather than expensive specialty hiking foods.

Hike Preparation

Preparation for hikes is essential. It can ensure the safety and enjoyment of the young women and prepare them to enjoy nature. Hikers should:

- Wear good shoes and socks, a hat, long pants (shorts won't protect legs), and a long-sleeved shirt.
- Bring a big garbage bag, which can be made into a raincoat by cutting a hole in the bottom for your head and a slit in each side for your arms. Garbage bags are also great for sliding on the snow if you find a patch.
- Bring and wear sunscreen.
- Bring enough water.
- Carry a first-aid kit containing bandages, ointment for insect bits, disinfectant, a bandana, petroleum jelly for chapped lips, aloe vera lotion for sunburn, and a whistle in case a hiker gets separated from the group. Leaders should have a group first-aid kit.

Stress the importance of staying together. Warn hikers of indigenous dangers like poison ivy, insects, or snakes. Place a leader in front of the line as well as at its back.

Complaints

Some hikers enjoy complaining. To help the young women enjoy their hike:

- Give each one a string and have her tie a knot for each complaint she verbalizes. Give prizes for the fewest knots.
- Each time a hiker complains, have her pick up a rock. Give prizes to those with the fewest rocks. Small prizes could include a key ring, a poem or story you have prepared, a certificate, and so forth.

GAMES

Scavenger hunt. This is as much fun for the leaders to play as it is for the campers. Make a list of items for the young women to find. The team finding everything on the list first gets to skip their next clean-up duty.

Bottle Launcher. To make a bottle launcher, you will need:

- Five feet of half-inch PVC pipe
- Three half-inch PVC caps
- Two ½-inch-by-½-inch-by-½-inch PVC tees (one not threaded; one with the middle leg threaded)
- Four inches of half-inch PVC nipple (threaded both ends)
- One automobile tire valve stem
- One can of PVC joint cement
- Several empty two-liter plastic pop bottles
- Tire pump

Cut the PVC pipe into one 32-inch piece, two 12-inch pieces, and one 4-inch piece. Drill a hole in one of the PVC caps large enough (about ⁹⁄₁₆) to accept the valve stem. Apply joint cement on connections and assemble as illustrated below.

After assembling, apply electrical tape around the end of the threaded nipple. Fill a two-liter bottle half full of water and attach it to the threaded nipple, push down, and turn clockwise to form a seal. Attach a tire pump to the valve stem and pump until the bottle launches into the air. Do not let anyone stand over the bottle while you are pumping!

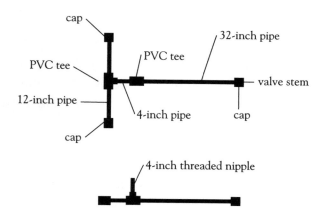

Water balloon or egg toss. Divide the young women into teams of two. Team members face one another, separated by only a step or two, and gently toss an egg or balloon back and forth. After each toss, they take one step back from their partner. The pair that is farthest apart when the egg or balloon breaks is the winner.

Ropes course. Many established camps have ropes courses. Certified counselors should direct these activities. Check with your local Boy Scouts for certified ropes course instructors, or contact the camp you'll be attending to see whom they recommend.

Egg drop. Give each young woman a hard-boiled egg, a sheet of typing paper, three straws, and a two-foot piece of masking tape. Their challenge is to create a cushion around the egg so that it can be dropped from fifty feet or more without breaking. The campers will have a great time comparing each other's creations and effectiveness.

Marshmallow fight. Give each group a bag of miniature marshmallows and each group member a foot-long section of half-inch PCV pipe. The groups shoot the marshmallows at each other, using their pipe sections like blowguns. Have the young women wear sunglasses to protect their eyes.

Arts and Crafts

Crafts can be a required part of camp. Two or three crafts can be taught simultaneously, allowing the young women to select which craft they want to do. A good camp craft is one that can be easily demonstrated and completed within an hour or two.

Invite artists or others with special talents to help teach crafts. At one camp, a professional watercolor instructor taught young women in her stake how to paint an outdoor scene using watercolor. As she demonstrated watercolor technique, she had the young women follow her step-by-step on their own watercolor paper. In less than two hours, each had completed an attractive outdoor watercolor scene.

To make arts and crafts memorable and to increase your success:

- Select age-appropriate activities.
- Help young women look at nature more closely and in detail.
- Teach young women to capture and interpret nature.
- Encourage young women to express their creativity.

Watercolor

Materials needed:
- White plastic, Styrofoam, or paper plates for palettes
- Paper towels and brown packing tape
- Paper cups or cans to hold water
- 140-pound watercolor paper
- Heavy cardboard (box sides) on which to tape 10-by-11-inch watercolor paper
- Brushes—one large half-inch flat brush, one No. 8 round brush, and one No. 4 brush (for details).
- Sponges (optional)
- Watercolors—ultramarine blue, burnt sienna, permanent alizarin crimson, gamboge yellow

To prepare watercolor paper, wet it with a sponge, brush off excess water, and tape all four sides to a piece of heavy cardboard. After it dries, you will be able to paint on it without it buckling.

To capture a beautiful sunset or a rosy dawn at camp:

1. Wet paper thoroughly again. Wet the brush with water and fill it with gamboge yellow and a touch of alizarin crimson, and then drop it along the bottom of the picture. Wash your brush quickly and add ultramarine blue and a touch of gamboge

yellow along the top. Now stop. Don't touch your brush to the paper again. Let the colors run together as they will, and allow the paper to dry thoroughly.

2. Wet the paper thoroughly again. This time, fill the brush with ultramarine blue and a little burnt sienna to make stormy clouds. Drop some of this mixture here and there about one-third of the way down the paper. Don't make these blobs too even; clouds come in different sizes. Put your brush down and let the water do the work. Don't touch it again until it dries.

3. To add grass or twigs along the bottom of the painting, mix the four colors together with just enough water to keep the mixture flowing. Stand up and paint a few twigs or grasses with the liner brush. (When you paint while standing up, you use your whole arm; your strokes are freer and your painting is more natural looking.) Dark green shrubbery can be added with a sponge. For dark green, mix together ultramarine blue and gamboge yellow and add a touch of burnt sienna.

Charcoal

Materials needed:
- Pencils—from 4B (softest) to HB (hardest), charcoal pencils, or charcoal sticks
- Student-grade drawing paper
- Gray scale (available at most art supply or craft stores)

When the young women hold a gray scale in front of the object or scene they're drawing, they can immediately see how many shades of light there are between the sunlit area and the shadow area. Charcoal drawings can be whimsical or even childish. The idea is not for the young women to recreate nature but to create their own interpretation of nature.

Acrylics

Materials needed:
- Waxed paper or plastic plates for palettes

- Medium-size round brushes
- Detergent-water (liquid detergent mixed with water) for cleaning brushes
- Sponges—cut or broken into smaller pieces
- Masking tape (to keep paint where you want it)
- Paper cups or cans to hold water
- Paper towels
- Acrylic paints—in bottles or tubes
- Rocks, wood, leather, fabric
- Animal picture books, insect field guidebooks

Whether painting on rock, wood, leather, or fabric, painting with acrylics can be a wonderfully imaginative activity. Let the shapes of rocks suggest the animals to be painted, or take ideas from an animal picture book. Have the young women use an insect field guidebook to create their own "bugs" by drawing on seedpods, rocks, twigs, and so forth. You might also bring along a reptile field guidebook and let the campers copy snake markings on twisted sticks and branches. Acrylics are also great for fabric painting, such as autographing the shoes of newfound friends.

Nature Jewelry

Materials needed:

- Jewelry wire—use colored wire or wire with a gold or silver finish (20-, 22-, 24-, and 26-gauge wire can be bent into many shapes)
- Small wire cutters
- Jewelry findings—pin backs, earring backs, clasps, chains, shells, polished rocks
- White glue for wood pieces and model glue for metal pieces
- A clear spray, sealer, or fingernail polish to finish porous materials

At camp, look for materials that have unusual shapes and subtle shades, that are not fragile, and that can be enhanced by jewelry findings. Use your imagination.

Wood Sculpture

Materials needed:

- Sandpaper—coarse and fine
- Wood glue or white glue
- Wood stain or shoe polish
- Spray furniture wax
- Small blocks of wood on which to mount sculptures

Begin with a theme, such as nature or Christmas. Young women could make small wooden figures for a nativity scene, using pieces of wood that resemble sheep, cattle, and people. At the seashore you may find useful pieces of weathered wood, while in the mountains you may find bits of gnarled roots that may suit your purposes.

Leaf Prints

Materials needed:

- Rubber brayers (available at art or craft stores) for each color of paint
- Acrylic paint and acrylic paint retarder (retarder slows the drying time slightly, allows more time for work)
- Waxed paper to use as palettes
- Fabric or paper

Find leaves of many shapes that have heavy veining on the back. Pour a puddle of paint onto a piece of waxed paper and mix well with a little retarder. Roll a brayer through it until paint is evenly distributed on the brayer. Then apply paint to the veined side of the leaf. Quickly place the leaf vein side down on fabric or paper and gently roll a clean brayer across the top of the leaf. Leaf prints can decorate T-shirts, stationery, notebooks, and canvas shoes.

Fish Prints

Materials needed:
- Whole fish (fresh from the store)
- Acrylic paints (use regular colors if you're printing T-shirts; if you want a fish print on black paper, use iridescent or metallic colors)
- Black paper or T-shirts
- Old brushes
- Fine, permanent ink pen (to add detail)
- Rubber gloves

Roughen the scales of a fish by gently stroking it against the grain with a spatula or credit card. Brush paint on the area of the fish you want to print. Then press and roll the fish on your fabric. Keep applying paint to the fish until you have painted every area you want to roll. Be careful not to add too much paint or you'll lose the shape of the fish. Use a fine-point permanent ink pen (available at craft stores) to add defining lines to your print.

Weaving

Materials needed:
- Cardboard squares from which to make a loom
- Craft stick to make a shuttle
- Yarn or twine
- Feathers, grasses, and pine needles that can be incorporated into a wall hanging (gathered from camp)

To weave, notch the top and bottom of the cardboard. Loop yarn or twine from top to bottom to create a weft. Attach the end of the weaving yarn or twine to the shuttle. Cut a notch in the end of the shuttle so the yarn can be slipped in with ease.

Put a spacer on each side to slightly raise the yarn or twine away from the cardboard, making it easier to weave. Spacers can be straight twigs gathered from camp.

Plant Press

Materials needed:
- Two eight-inch squares of thin plywood
- Four long bolts with wing nuts and washers
- Newsprint end roll (often available free at small-town newspapers)
- Leaves, flowers, and plants (gathered at camp)

To make a plant press, lay the two boards together and drill holes in the corners. Lay two or three paper towels on one of the boards, followed by several sheets of newspaper. Then lay the leaves and plant material on the newspaper, covering them with several sheets of newspaper and two or three paper towels. Place the other board on top, connect the corners together with wing nuts, and tighten. Continue tightening the wing nuts a little each day as the leaves, flowers, and plants dry out. To reduce drying time, carefully change the paper towels every other day.

It takes about a week for the pressed leaves, flowers, and plants to lose their moisture. So during a Young Women activity after camp, arrange the pressed items in picture frames or cover them with page sealer plastic and add them to stationery or bookmarks.

Leather

Materials needed:
- Thick leather
- Leather punch
- Leather stamps
- Mallets
- Tracing paper (optional)

Leatherworking is a time-tested camp craft. Many supplies and ideas for tooling leather are available at leather stores, but rather than purchase leather, use old purses, leather coats, and leather jeans, or get a chamois skin from the grocery store. To make small purses, cut out pieces of leather, punch holes around the edges of the pieces, and lace them together with leather lacing.

To stamp thick leather, sketch or trace a design and transfer it to the leather. Dampen the leather with water, place a leather stamp on it, and pound it with a mallet. Try to pound the mallet with the same force each time to get a uniform design.

Beads

Materials needed:
- Beads of different sizes and colors
- Wire, gut, or beading line (boondoggle)
- Paper or plastic plate or bowl to hold loose beads
- Egg cartons to separate colors
- Long beading needle if you are using seed beads

Here are some ways you can easily make handmade beads:
- Seal small, dry pasta shapes by spraying them with sealer; then paint them with acrylic.
- Make beads from polymer clay (if an oven is available).
- Use wooden beads that have been wood burned.
- Use materials found at camp, such as seeds, tiny pinecones, and so forth.
- Use colorful magazine pages and Mod Podge—a water-based glue, sealer, and finish—to make paper beads. For each bead, cut a long, banner-shaped triangle from colored paper. Coat the triangle with Mod Podge, and then roll it around a thin knitting needle to dry.

Use a toothpick to paint flowers on wooden beads. To do

this, dip a toothpick in a puddle of acrylic paint and make a dot on the bead. Surround that dot with six dots of another color and you have a flower.

Rubbings

Materials needed:
- Pencils
- Paper

Simply put a leaf under a piece of paper and gently rub a pencil over the top of it. The details of the leaf will make a beautiful keepsake.

Sand Clay

Materials needed:
- 1 cup sand
- ⅓ cup cornstarch
- ¾ cup liquid starch

Mix the above ingredients and cook over medium heat until the mixture forms a ball. Dump it out on a flat surface and knead it until it is workable. Sand clay makes good sand sculptures.

NATURE CENTER

The main purpose of a nature center is to focus the young women's attention on nature. A nature center is a resource area for information on nature and certification skills. It includes books on plants, animals, weather, and stars, as well as posters, games, hands-on activities, magazine articles, and exhibits that can help the campers learn about the area around them and pass off certification skills.

The nature center is generally a quiet place geared toward learning and reflection. It's a place where those with special interests can feel at home. During free time or at specified times of the day, a nature mentor might be on duty to answer questions and pique the interest of the young women.

Activities such as slug races and nature crafts can be held at the nature center. The center is also a good place for the young women to attune their senses to nature and share their discoveries of the outdoors. Center exhibits are to be touched, smelled, and experienced. The center should also feature nature music or sounds. The nature center can also be a spiritual place where the young women develop an appreciation for God's creations.

Exhibits

National and state park visitors centers, societies such as the National Audubon Society, and local museums can supply pamphlets, posters, information, and small exhibits for your nature center. Check out your local library as well. Most of these items cost little or nothing. Sometimes pet stores will loan out animals and reptiles for exhibit. Here are some exhibit ideas:

Earth. Earth exhibits might include rocks, shells, posters, and fossils. Activities might include hunting for fossils, panning for fool's gold, constructing mock volcanoes, hunting rocks, or making rock jewelry.

Plants. Plant exhibits might include live plants, tree bark, edible berries, poisonous plants, natural dyes, pressed flower books, drawings and posters, items made from plants, and plant-identification games.

Animals. Animal exhibits might include hides, hoofs, horns, skulls, plaster track casts, posters, drawings, empty wasp nests, ant farms, bug and butterfly collections, feathers, stuffed animals, and live animals. Snakes, rats, lizards, frogs, tame squirrels, and rabbits make popular exhibits. Be careful to see that animals don't get stressed out or handled too much.

If your camp is surrounded by wild animals, build a "track

CLOUD TYPES

Delicate, wispy, high-level clouds are called *Cirrus*. They are formed from ice particles.

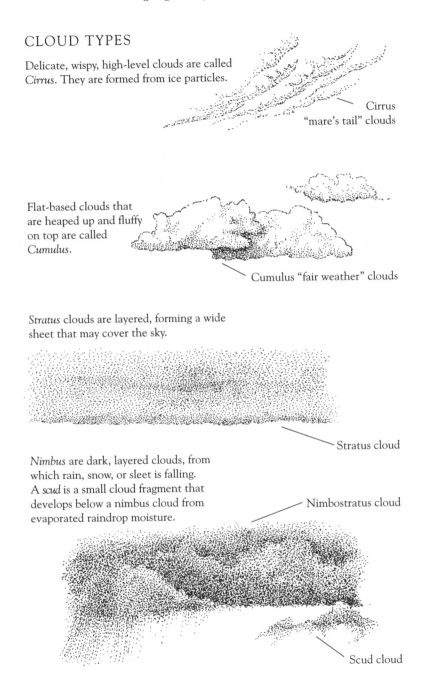

Cirrus
"mare's tail" clouds

Flat-based clouds that are heaped up and fluffy on top are called *Cumulus*.

Cumulus "fair weather" clouds

Stratus clouds are layered, forming a wide sheet that may cover the sky.

Stratus cloud

Nimbus are dark, layered clouds, from which rain, snow, or sleet is falling. A *scud* is a small cloud fragment that develops below a nimbus cloud from evaporated raindrop moisture.

Nimbostratus cloud

Scud cloud

138

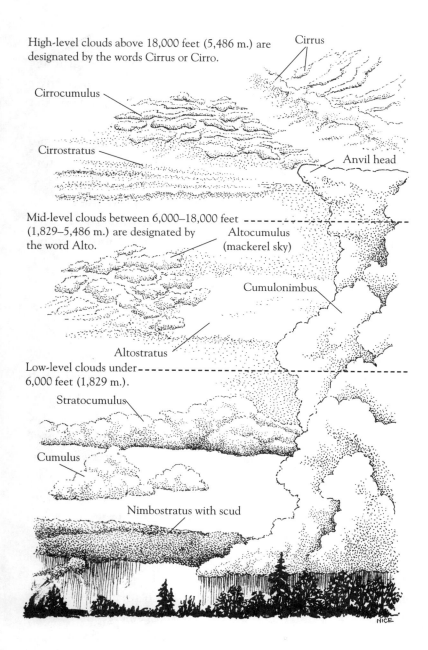

High-level clouds above 18,000 feet (5,486 m.) are designated by the words Cirrus or Cirro.

Cirrus

Cirrocumulus

Cirrostratus

Anvil head

Mid-level clouds between 6,000–18,000 feet (1,829–5,486 m.) are designated by the word Alto.

Altocumulus (mackerel sky)

Cumulonimbus

Altostratus

Low-level clouds under 6,000 feet (1,829 m.).

Stratocumulus

Cumulus

Nimbostratus with scud

trap" out of firm mud. Put food in the middle that will attract animals. For example, deer feed on berries, buds, and twigs. Birds, squirrels, and other small animals eat bread crumbs, grains, and nuts. As they come to feed they will leave their tracks in the mud. The tracks can be cast in plaster of Paris and used for an exhibit.

Weather. Your weather exhibit might include posters, drawings, a weather station, and mock clouds made out of cotton. Activities might include recording weather observations, classifying cloud types, and predicting the next day's weather.

Stars. An astronomy exhibit could feature star charts, posters, and models. Star gazing with binoculars and telescopes is a lot of fun.

PINECONE LEGEND

The Pinecone Legend is a tradition at the Brighton Girls Camp. During their last program at camp, the young women are given a pinecone on yarn to wear as a necklace and to take home as a memento. But before the young women receive their pinecones, leaders read or paraphrase the following story:

"Before you leave camp today, take a minute to look around you. Notice how beautiful our surroundings are: the majestic peaks, the streams, the wildflowers, the green meadows, and the animal life. Many beautiful creations of our Father in Heaven surround us. Note particularly the many pine trees around us. See how tall, firm, beautiful, and straight they grow. They represent to us great strength and determination.

"Each new season, the pine tree forms cones at the tops of its branches. These pinecones eventually fall to the ground and become lodged in the soft dirt, after which they begin sending out roots deep into the soil. New pine trees emerge, and as they grow, they battle the elements: severe windstorms, driving rain, heavy snowfall, and hot sun. Only the strong, determined, and best-rooted trees will survive and grow to maturity. As they do so, they grow stronger and more beautiful.

"We should try to pattern our lives after the pine trees. When we face challenges, we need to realize that if we are strong and determined, we will become as beautiful as the pine trees.

"As you continue to grow, reach toward your Heavenly Father and put your trust in him. As long as there are trees in tiny seeds, there will be miracles on earth."

SECRET SISTER

Secret Sisters is a fun activity that can foster love and friendship among young women. Each camper is assigned another young woman to serve through the week. Secret Sisters do anonymous acts of service, write notes, give small gifts, and so forth. A daily theme may be announced at the morning flag ceremony. Secret Sisters reveal their identities on the last day of camp.

AWARDS

One of the goals of camp is to build self-worth and create lasting memories. Here are a few ideas you may want to consider.

Badges. Leaders can award badges similar to Boy Scout merit badges, rewarding young women for learning skills. The young women would be proud to receive badges for cooking, pitching tents, learning nature skills, and making crafts.

Beads. To provide a lasting reminder of camp and to serve as an incentive, beads can be awarded for various accomplishments and activities. For example, award a bead for passing off certification items, keeping camp clean, and learning skills. As young women check in, give them a bead string.

Certificates. Make camp certificates by hand or with a computer program. Here are some possible ideas:
- Smokey Bear—for demonstrating fire safety

- Red Cross—for aiding someone who was hurt
- Trailblazer—for learning compass skills or being the best hiker
- Insect Inspector—for catching the most bugs
- Reptile Wrangler—for catching a nonpoisonous snake
- Camp Musician—for making up the best song
- Marshmallow Chef—for making the best toasted marshmallows
- Flower Identification—for identifying the most flowers
- Above and Beyond—for doing the most for others

SECRET SISTER PROFILE
(all kinds of good things for my Secret Sister to know about me!)

Name _____ Birthday _____ Ward _____

Phone _____ Address _____

There are _____ people in my family

Their names are _____

Some cool things about my family are _____

_____

_____

My favorite thing to do with my family is _____

My favorite school subject _____ Why? _____

_____

Favorite: color _____ song _____

movie _____ food _____

sport _____ book _____

dessert _____ TV show _____

scripture _____

Why? _____

_____

I'm happiest when _____

_____

I would describe myself as _____

_____

I'm a good friend because _____

_____

My favorite thing to do with my friends is _____

_____

A place I would like to visit is _____

Some hobbies and interests I have are _____

_____

_____

Something unique about me is _____

_____

When I grow up I want to _____

_____

_____

Things I like most about camp are _____

CHAPTER 8

EVENING PROGRAMS

Camp evening programs, such as campfire sharing, pageants, and group singing, help create unity. As the young women participate together, their friendships and appreciation for each other and their leaders blossom. Some of the best camp memories are created in the flickering firelight.

CAMPFIRE SHARING

Testimony meeting. Testimony meetings on the last night can be a wonderful opportunity for the young women to share what is in their hearts.

Open-ended sentences. These are sentences that help the young women share around a campfire. Many will not say anything if you simply ask them to participate. Giving them an open-ended sentence to complete helps focus their thoughts. Here are some examples:

- My favorite activity today was . . .
- What I discovered about myself at camp was . . .
- My favorite camp activity was . . .
- My favorite camp song is . . .
- The most important thing I learned at camp is . . .
- A camp activity I would like to do with my family is . . .

Comfort in nature. Have each young woman share a comfort she gets from nature. Here are some examples:

- Wood makes houses.
- Water makes drinks.
- Rocks become jewelry and houses.
- Fire makes warmth.
- Mud becomes mortar.

Share helping hands. Have the young women talk about kind deeds done at camp. This helps the young women realize things that they can do to serve and ways they can share with their group. Examples include:

- Leaders planned an activity.
- One young woman helped another cross a stream.
- One young woman shared her water.
- Someone left a kind note under another young woman's pillow.
- A young woman put her arm around someone who needed comforting.

Create a story. Have a young woman start a story. After a few minutes, a second young woman continues the story. The young women continuing taking turns, adding to the story when their turn comes.

The story could be your story of organizing camp. For example, "Four camp leaders met in January to plan summer camp. They worked and planned for the wonderful occasion that would take place with all the campers in the _____ branch, ward, or stake." When the leaders end, the young women join in and tell their experiences.

Paper bag skits. Give each group a paper bag with props in it. Props could include several handy objects, such as scissors, a spoon, a mirror, and so forth. The young women then create a skit using the props.

NIGHT PAGEANTS

Night pageants can be a highlight of camp. These programs can be built around themes such as:

Fantasy. This has been a tradition for more than fifty years at the Brighton Girls Camp near Salt Lake City for twelve- and thirteen-year-olds. One group told a story about "Brownies"— tiny, make-believe people who lived in the woods (for the full story, go to www.campingwithdian.com/browniestory.htm). After the story, the young women joined hands and toured "Brownie Land."

Unbeknownst to the young women, the leaders had prepared the tour beforehand by building several Brownie attractions: a flat rock where the Brownies had written "welcome" with sticks and twigs, a small beach scene by a stream, and a tiny swimming pool made of aluminum foil. Another stop was a Brownie "pipe organ": an area where several tall trees grew together and near which a hidden leader played flute music. The last stop featured a special treat made by the Brownies: brownies.

Afterward, the group gathered around a campfire, singing to the Brownies and asking them, "If we sing a song, will you sing a song?" Leaders hiding in the trees answered, singing a camp song with high, tiny voices.

Spiritual. At an effective night pageant in Oregon, Youth Camp Leaders were in charge of stations during a night hike. They created songs, costumes, and readings, which they presented at four separate stations.

The young women held hands as they walked through the woods, stopping at each station to hear a spiritual story and song. The camp's theme was, "We are daughters of a King." As the hike ended, the young women were greeted by a priesthood leader dressed as a king. He welcomed them into an assembly

146

area with benches and a stage that had been draped with white sheets.

A group of YCLs on the stage greeted the group by singing beautiful, spiritual songs. The young women felt as if they had been welcomed into heaven. After all the young women had gathered, the entire group sang songs. This experience created a memory that will last forever.

Patriotic. Select a period in the history of the country and create stories and messages around an event that will help increase the young women's love for their country. You could select one of the following themes for your pageant:

- History of the national flag
- The national anthem
- The Restoration
- The pioneer trek west
- Patriotic events from the nation's history

Music

Camp without music isn't camp. Music provides the basis for many fun activities at campfires, on hikes, in skits, and during spiritual times. Instruments can add a special touch. Find out what portable instruments the young women and leaders play and encourage them to bring them to camp. Guitars or ukuleles are a must. If no one plays, encourage someone to take lessons and learn camp songs. Young women often continue singing camp songs long after camp ends, and many even sing them to their children.

Theme songs. These songs are made up just for camp or for an individual group. It's fun to have each camp group make up a song to share at a campfire. Have groups select a tune and make up words about their camp experiences. You can also give them two items from nature to include in their song, such as a pinecone, rock, or branch.

Rounds. Round songs are simple songs sung in groups. Each group begins at a different point. Rounds can be lots of fun.

Fun songs. These songs often have actions to accompany the lyrics, and they may have many verses.

Spiritual songs and hymns. Hymns and spiritual songs set a serious, reflective mood and are usually sung around the campfire and during evening programs.

Folk and traditional songs. Folks songs are familiar songs that are fun to sing. The *Young Women Camp Songs* booklet contains some great songs, as does a CD of Brighton Girls Camp songs. For a copy of the CD and an accompanying songbook with guitar chords, go to www.campingwithdian.com/campsongs.htm.

CHAPTER 9

RECIPES

STICK COOKING

BREAD ON A STICK

1 dowel or roasting stick for each person
1 box Bisquick mix
1 cup water
½ cup (one stick) butter or margarine
1 cup honey or jam

Using the end of the stick, make a little well in the open box of Bisquick. Pour 1 tablespoon of water into the well. Place the stick in the well and begin stirring until a small ball of dough forms around the stick. Lift the stick out of the box and press the dough firmly around the end of the stick. Pass the box and water to the next person to repeat.

Grill the dough stick over a bed of hot coals and turn often. When your bread is golden brown and cooked throughout, slide it off the stick and slather it with butter, honey, or jam. Sit back and enjoy until the box makes its way again to you. A large box of Bisquick makes more than twenty servings.

Figure 9–1. *Make a well in the Bisquick.*

Figure 9–2. *Pour water into the well.*

Figure 9–3. *Stir with the end of the stick to form a ball of dough.*

Figure 9–4. *Mold the dough onto the stick to cook it over coals.*

MEAT LOAF ON A STICK

1 dowel or roasting stick for each person
1 one-gallon, plastic, reclosable bag
1 cup cornflakes
1 pound ground beef
1 egg
½ onion, chopped
1 teaspoon salt
⅛ teaspoon pepper
½ teaspoon prepared mustard

Pour cornflakes into a one-gallon, plastic, reclosable bag and squeeze to crush. Add ground beef, egg, onion, salt, pepper, and

Figure 9–5. *Cooking meat loaf on a stick is simple and quick.*

mustard to the bag. Repeatedly squeeze the bag until the contents are well mixed. For each person, wrap a small quantity of this mixture around the end of a stick, making an oblong shape. Wrap foil around the mixture and part of the stick and seal it using the drugstore wrap (page 83). Grill over a bed of hot coals for twenty to twenty-five minutes, turning often to cook evenly. Serves three to four people.

TERIYAKI MEAT STICKS

6 to 8 skewers
1 one-gallon, plastic, reclosable bag
2 pounds sirloin steak, sliced across the grain to ⅛-inch
    thick (ask your butcher to slice the meat for you, or
    partially freeze it so you can slice it more easily)
Teriyaki marinade (below)

Place steak slices in the reclosable bag, cover with marinade, and place in a cooler overnight. Thread meat onto skewers. Grill, turning occasionally, until meat is done. Makes six to eight kabobs.

Figure 9–6.
*Crowd-pleasing
Teriyaki Meat
Sticks.*

Teriyaki Marinade

This is an excellent marinade for meat sticks, spare ribs, chicken, and steak.

1 cup soy sauce
½ cup sugar
½ cup water
½ tablespoon fresh ginger, shredded
1 clove garlic, peeled and crushed
2 green onions, chopped
1 tablespoon sesame seed oil

In a medium saucepan, heat soy sauce, sugar, and water, boiling until sugar dissolves (about five minutes). Add ginger, garlic, green onions, and sesame seed oil. Pour into a one-pint jar, cover, and place in a cooler. This recipe makes enough marinade for three pounds of meat.

HAM SUPREME KABOBS

6 skewers
12 thin ham slices
½ cup prepared mustard
1 six-ounce can whole olives
1 five-ounce jar cocktail onions, drained
6 cherry tomatoes

Spread each ham slice with mustard. Fold into bite-sized pieces (mustard side in) and thread on skewers, alternating with olives, onions, and tomatoes. Grill over a bed of hot coals, turning often, until ham is warmed through. Serves six.

ROASTED CINNAMON-SUGAR APPLE PIE ON A STICK

4 dowels or roasting sticks
1 small bowl or plastic bag
1 cup sugar
1 tablespoon cinnamon
4 apples (the best apples are Jonathan, Rome, or Granny Smith because the skin peels off easily when heated)

In a bowl or plastic bag, mix the cinnamon and sugar and set aside. Push a stick or dowel securely through an apple. Roast the apple two to three inches above a bed of hot coals and turn frequently. As the apple cooks, the skin will turn brown and juice will dribble out. When the skin is loose, remove the apple from the coals but leave it on the stick. Peel off the skin, being careful not to burn yourself, and roll the apple in the cinnamon-sugar mixture. Return the apple to roast over the coals. The cinnamon and sugar will form a glaze on the apple. Be careful not to get the apple so close to the fire that it burns. Remove the apple from the coals and let it cool. Slice into thin pieces and enjoy. Serves four.

SHAGGY DOGS

8 sticks
1 sixteen-ounce package large marshmallows
1 cup chocolate or caramel syrup, heated
1 cup shredded coconut

Roast each marshmallow on a stick over a bed of hot coals until it turns golden brown. Dip it into warm syrup and roll it in coconut. Serves eight or more.

ALUMINUM FOIL COOKING

BUTTERNUT SQUASH WITH APPLES

18-inch-wide heavy-duty aluminum foil
2 tablespoons oil
1 butternut squash, peeled and cut into ½-inch slices
2 cooking apples, peeled and sliced
¼ cup (½ stick) butter or margarine
¼ cup brown sugar
½ teaspoon cinnamon
½ teaspoon nutmeg

Cut four squares of foil and brush with oil. Place one-quarter of the squash and one-quarter of the apple slices on each square. Top each mixture with one tablespoon butter and one tablespoon brown sugar. Sprinkle with cinnamon and nutmeg. Seal, using the drugstore wrap (page 83). Bake on grill or hot coals, turning occasionally, for about forty-five minutes, or until tender. Serves six to eight.

CORN ON THE COB

18-inch-wide heavy-duty aluminum foil
Ears of corn with husks
Butter or margarine, softened
Salt
Pepper

Peel back the husks from the ears and remove the silk. Spread on butter, and season with salt and pepper. Pull the husks over the ears and wrap individually in aluminum foil. Cook on a bed of hot coals for ten to fifteen minutes, turning frequently. Always cook corn with the husks on to prevent it from burning. This corn is much sweeter than corn cooked in water.

HOBO DINNER

18-inch-wide heavy-duty aluminum foil
2 carrots, peeled and thinly sliced
2 medium potatoes, peeled and thinly sliced
2 onions, sliced
1 pound ground beef, shaped into four patties (chicken
      breast or fish fillets can be substituted)
1 teaspoon salt
½ teaspoon pepper

Cut four squares of foil. Divide vegetables into four equal portions. Layer with half the carrots, potatoes, and onions. Then add the ground beef and layer on the remaining onions, potatoes, and carrots. Season with salt and pepper. Seal using the drugstore wrap (page 83), and cook on a bed of hot coals for fifteen minutes on each side. Serves four.

BANANA BOAT

18-inch-wide heavy-duty aluminum foil
1 banana, unpeeled
Miniature marshmallows
Milk chocolate chips or broken candy bars

Cut a slit lengthwise about two-thirds of the way through the banana from the stem to the base. Fill the slit with marshmallows and chocolate chips or pieces of a chocolate bar. Wrap in foil and cook on hot coals for five minutes or until the chocolate and marshmallows have melted. If you leave the boats in the coals too long, the bananas will liquefy. Serve as a snack, a dessert, or a treat around the campfire. You can also create a fruit "banana boat" by using maraschino cherries, shredded coconut, nuts, and pineapple.

GRILLING

GRILLED FISH

2 tablespoons olive oil
2 large (½- to 1-inch thick) fish fillets
½ teaspoon salt
⅛ teaspoon pepper

Camp stove. In a large skillet, heat oil; add fish and season with salt and pepper. Cook for 2½ to 4½ minutes on each side, or until fish flakes and is opaque. Serves two.

Grill. Heat grill and brush with oil. When hot, add fish fillets and cook 2½ to 4½ minutes per side. To prevent fish from flaking and falling into the coals, place a strip of pierced, oiled foil on the grill and lay the fish on the foil. Be careful not to overcook. When fish flakes easily, it is fully cooked. Serves two.

Dutch oven lid. Place the lid of a twelve-inch Dutch oven upside down on a lid holder over twelve to fifteen hot coals. Preheat the lid for five minutes. Brush oil on hot lid, add fish, and season with salt and pepper. Cook 2½ to 4½ minutes on each side, or until the fillets are evenly browned and flake easily. Serves two.

GRILLED VEGETABLES

¼ cup garlic and herb butter or margarine, melted
1 zucchini squash, cut in lengthwise slices
1 yellow squash, cut in lengthwise slices
3 large white or red onions, sliced ½-inch thick
2 blanched artichokes (with centers removed), cut into 4
    sections
8 large mushroom caps, halved
½ teaspoon salt
¼ teaspoon pepper

If your grill has wide spaces between the ribs, cut the

vegetables large enough to prevent their falling into the fire, or grill them on a piece of pierced, oiled foil. Most fresh vegetables in season are good for grilling. Brush with them with olive oil and turn them over halfway through cooking.

Grill. Brush vegetables with butter or margarine and place on the hot grill. Grill on each side for five to ten minutes to brown and soften. Add salt and pepper and serve. Serves four.

Dutch oven lid. Place the lid of a twelve-inch Dutch oven upside down on a lid holder over twelve to fifteen hot coals. Preheat the lid for about ten minutes. Brush vegetables with butter or margarine and arrange on the lid. Cook for ten minutes on each side until browned and soft. Add salt and pepper and serve. Serves four.

HAMBURGERS

1 one-gallon, plastic, reclosable bag
1 pound of ground beef, chicken, pork, or turkey
1 egg
½ teaspoon salt
Dash pepper
½ medium onion, chopped
Spices as desired
Bread or cracker crumbs
Milk to moisten

Combine meat, egg, salt, pepper, onion, spices, bread or cracker crumbs, and milk in the reclosable bag. Push air out of the bag and seal. Squeeze to mix thoroughly. Divide into fourths and shape into patties. Grill over hot coals, turning over after five minutes, to desired doneness. Serve with your choice of toppings below. Serves four.

Toppings:

Chili peppers with Monterey Jack cheese
Grilled onions with spinach and bacon

Lettuce, tomatoes, onions, and avocado slices
Onions and green peppers
Pepperoni
Shredded cheese
Tomato slices with mozzarella cheese
Tomatoes, garlic paste, and fresh basil

Sauces:

Barbecue sauce
Herbed butter
Chili
Marinara sauce
Cocktail sauce
Nacho cheese sauce

NOVELTY COOKING

MEAT LOAF IN AN ONION

18-inch-wide heavy-duty aluminum foil
1 one-gallon, plastic, reclosable bag
1 pound lean ground beef
1 egg
¼ cup cracker crumbs
¼ cup tomato sauce
½ teaspoon salt
⅛ teaspoon pepper
½ teaspoon dry mustard
4 large onions, peeled and halved

Combine ground beef, egg, cracker crumbs, tomato sauce, salt, pepper, and dry mustard in the reclosable bag. Mix by squeezing and set aside. Cut onions in half horizontally and remove center part of onion, leaving a three-quarter-inch-thick shell. Divide meat mixture into four portions and roll into balls. Place in the center of the four onion halves and put onions back together. Wrap each onion in foil using the drug-store wrap (page 83). Cook over a bed of hot coals for fifteen to twenty minutes per side. Serves four.

Figure 9–7. *Squeeze your orange in a bag and drink with a straw.*

ORANGE JUICE IN A BAG

Remove the pulp from a juicy orange using the method described on page 96. Place the fruit inside a one-quart, plastic, reclosable bag. Remove as much air as you can from the bag and seal. Squeeze the fruit at the bottom to release juice. Then turn the bag on its side. Place your hand in the center of the bag on the bottom and loosely gather it to the top, leaving enough room for the juice to flow to the empty side as you continue to squeeze the bottom of the bag. Open the top of the bag and insert a straw where the juice is collecting. This is the freshest squeezed juice you can have.

APPLE WALKING SALAD

This is one of my favorite snacks to take on a hike.

2 tablespoons chunky or plain peanut butter
2 tablespoons raisins
1 apple, cored
1 tablespoon lemon juice

In a small bowl, mix peanut butter and raisins. Slice the top off of an apple and brush lemon juice onto all cut areas. Spoon the mixture into the center and place the apple back together. Serves one.

PUDDING CONE

1 three-ounce package instant pudding, any flavor
Milk
1 ice cream cone per person

Prepare pudding as directed on package. Serve in empty ice cream cones. Top with marshmallows and a cherry. Serves six to eight. Potato salad, gelatin, pear halves, and other foods are also fun to eat in ice cream cones.

KICK-THE-CAN ICE CREAM

Making ice cream outdoors provides both recreation and a cool treat. It also creates fun memories.

1 one-pound coffee can with plastic lid
1 cup whole milk
1 cup heavy cream
⅓ cup sugar
2 tablespoons flavored syrup, such as chocolate or strawberry
1 No. 10 can with plastic lid
Small bag ice, cubed (not crushed)
½ cup rock salt

Add milk, cream, sugar, and syrup to the small can. Do not fill the can more than half full with liquids or the ice cream will not freeze well. Cover the small can with a plastic lid and place it inside the large can. Fill the bottom half of the space between the two cans with ice, add rock salt, fill the rest of the space with ice, and put on the plastic lid.

Ask two people to roll the can back and forth to each other

Figure 9–8. *Kick-the-Can Ice Cream is a frozen treat made in a tin can.*

for ten minutes. Remove the lids and scrape the ice cream from the sides of the small can. Stir the mixture. If the ice cream needs to freeze longer, pour the water out of the large can, set the small can back inside the large can, and add more ice and rock salt as needed. The ice cream will be ready when there is about a half-inch of frozen mixture on the sides of the can; the remaining mixture will still be in near-liquid form. (Adding chopped frozen fruit will speed the freezing time). Scrape down the frozen ice cream and stir it into the liquid ice cream to create the right consistency. Makes about two cups.

BALL-TOSS ICE CREAM

This is a great group activity. Divide into pairs and make one recipe per pair.

Newspapers
Duct tape
2 one-quart, plastic, reclosable bags
2 one-gallon, plastic, reclosable bags
1 cup whole milk

I cup heavy cream
⅓ cup sugar
½ cup rock salt
Ice, cubed (not crushed)

Combine milk, cream, and sugar in one-quart bag, and then squeeze as much air out of the bag as you can. Close the bag and place it inside another one-quart bag. Place the ice cream mixture inside a one-gallon bag. Fill the area between with ice and rock salt, alternately. Seal the bag and place it inside the second one-gallon bag.

Open up sections of a newspaper as if you were reading the center pages. Stack the newspapers on top of each other until you have a half-inch-high stack. Place the ice cream bag in a corner of the papers. Lift the corner and roll until you have covered the entire bag with newspaper. Fold in both sides and continue rolling. Repeat until all newspapers are used. Tape the newspapers shut with duct tape. Secure the "ball" on all sides so that it will retain its shape when tossed. Have each pair of young women toss the ice cream ball back and forth for fifteen to twenty minutes. Makes about two cups.

SOLAR COOKING

LASAGNA

I quart spaghetti sauce
½ pound ricotta cheese
½ pound shredded mozzarella cheese
Parmesan cheese
½ pound uncooked lasagna noodles
Onion and garlic to taste

In the bottom of a roaster pan, pour one-third of the spaghetti sauce. Layer uncooked noodles with ricotta cheese in the bottom of the pan. Add half the shredded mozzarella.

Repeat to make a second layer. Top with remaining spaghetti sauce and Parmesan cheese. Cover and bake for three hours. For meat lasagna, brown one pound of ground beef with onion and garlic in a solar cooker for 1½ hours. Drain, add meat to spaghetti sauce, and prepare as above. Serves four.

CUSTARD

2 eggs
2 cups of milk
3 to 4 tablespoons of sugar
¼ teaspoon salt
1 teaspoon vanilla
Nutmeg to taste

Mix together all ingredients; sprinkle with nutmeg. Cover and bake in glass custard dishes about 1½ hours. Custards will bake more evenly when placed in a pan with boiling water. Remove and let cool before serving. Serves two.

INDEX

of outdoor, 75; in high altitude, 76; timing of, 76–77; without recipes, 77–78; with sticks, 78–80, 149–53; on spits, 80–81; in aluminum foil, 82, 154–55; in Dutch ovens, 89–92; over grills, 93–95, 156–58; food inside of food, 96–97, 158; inside a paper bag, 98; inside leaves, 98–99; in cardboard box ovens, 99–101; in pie-tin ovens, 101–102; in solar cookers, 102–9, 162–63; in reflector ovens, 109–12; in pits, 112–15
Cooking bags, 19
CooKit, 103
Cooks, 8
Coolers: burlap, 38–39; commercial, 39
Corn on the Cob, 154
Crafts: specialist in, 5; types of, 128–36
Custard, 163

Destination, choosing, 2
Dishwashing station, 42–44
Drugstore wrap, 84
Dutch ovens: history of, 84–85; types of, 85–87; seasoning, 87–88; cleaning and storing, 88–89; accessories for, 89; cooking with, 89–92

Eating area, 41–42
Egg drop, 128
Embroidery hoops, 20
Equipment: specialist for, 5; obtaining, 18; care for, 44–45
Equipment list: general, 27–28; personal, 28–33
Exhibits, nature, 137, 140

Fire. *See* Campfire
First aid: specialist for, 5–6; kits for, 54
Fish, cooking, 95, 156
Fish prints, 132
Flint and steel, 64

Food: specialist for, 5; storing, 35, 37–40; preparation area for, 41; for backpacking, 125. *See also* Cooking
Fuel tablets, 71
Fuels: liquid, 44, 69–71; other, 71–72

Games, 126–28
Gasoline, unleaded, 71
Gloves, heatproof, 21
Grills: improvising, 10–11; cooking over, 93–95, 156–57
Ground cloth, 26
Guylines, 25

Ham Supreme Kabobs, 152–53
Hamburgers, grilled, 157–58
Hammers, 26
Hatchets, 44–45
Heaters, portable, 44
Hiking: planning around, 3; specialist in, 5; types of, 119–22, 146–47; guidelines for, 126–27
Hobo Dinner, 82, 155

Ice Cream: Kick-the-Can, 160–61; Ball-Toss, 161–62
Improvisation, 10
Insects: in food, 20; repelling, 29–30, 56; protection from, 35

Jewelry, nature, 131–32
Journals, 116–18

Kabobs, 79–80, 151–52
Kindness, acts of, 145
Knives, 44–45

Lasagna, 162–63
Latrines, 51–52
Leaf cooking, 98–99
Leaf prints, 132
Leatherwork, 134–35
Log bench, 41

Magnifying glass, 64
Marshmallow fight, 128
Matches, waterproof, 63
Meal preparation, 6–8, 16
Meatloaf: on a stick, 150–51; in an

ABOUT THE AUTHOR

Dian Thomas, "America's First Lady of Creativity," is a best-selling author, professional speaker, and television personality. Her *New York Times* best-selling book, *Roughing It Easy*, has sold more than a million copies. Follow-up books include *Backyard Roughing It Easy* and *Recipes for Roughing It Easy*. Each of these volumes has helped millions of campers and enthusiasts share Dian's love of the outdoors.

Dian has performed her magic on *The Tonight Show*, *Good Morning America*, *The Martin Short Show*, *Phil Donahue*, and *Sally Jessy Raphael*. From her network television appearances as a regular member of NBC's *Today Show* for eight years, Dian created the book *Today's Tips for Easy Living*. She produced the best-seller *Fun at Home* from her six years of weekly appearances on ABC's *Home Show*. Her other best-selling book, *Holiday Fun Year-Round*, has become a classic for families looking for innovative ideas for holiday celebrations.

Dian's career began humbly in a national forest in southern Utah, where she assisted her father, a forest ranger. Her childhood memories of her first formal camping experience led to the creation of *Roughing It Easy at Girls Camp*. The core of Dian's many accomplishments dates back to her years at Brighton Girls Camp, where she met counselors, leaders, and staff who shaped the experiences that would change her life forever.

www.dianthomas.com, campingwithdian.com, craftswithdian.com